LOVING THE GOD WHO LOVES YOU

Loving the God Who Loves You

FLOYD McCLUNG

KINGSWAY PUBLICATIONS
EASTBOURNE

First published 1993

Unless otherwise indicated, biblical quotations are from the
Revised Standard Version © 1946, 1952, 1971, 1973 by
the Division of Education and Ministry of the National
Council of the Churches of Christ in the USA.

ISBN 0 86065 9453

Produced by Bookprint Creative Services
P.O. Box 827, BN23 6NX, England for
KINGSWAY PUBLICATIONS LTD
Lottbridge Drove, Eastbourne, E Sussex BN23 6NT.
Printed in Great Britain by Clay's Ltd, St Ives plc
Typesetting by Servant Publications, Michigan, USA,
and used by arrangement

To Sally, my closest friend and companion for twenty-five years

Contents

Foreword

Foreword

When I first met Floyd McClung over a quarter of a century ago, I was impressed by this tall, athletic teenager who was an obvious leader. But most of all, I recognized that he was a young man with a quest to know God.

This quest has been the theme of Floyd's life. From his knowledge of God has flowed the fruit of service to his God and to countless people—needy, suffering and alone—from Amsterdam to Afghanistan, from California to Calcutta.

As I read Floyd's book I found myself being swept upwards into the majestic infiniteness and yet tenderness of the creator God. This book will inspire you to an enrichment of your life through your daily walk with the Lord, and a contentment and fulfillment in your service towards God and man.

Loren Cunningham

Introduction

It was almost 2000 years ago that Jesus entered the human race in a small Middle Eastern town. He was born of a poor family, a member of an ethnic minority group, and he lived only thirty-three short years.

Though he lived in poverty and was raised in obscurity, and though he received no formal education and did not possess wealth or widespread influence, and though he did not travel extensively, this one man's life has changed the course of history and the lives of millions of people.

His infancy frightened a king; in childhood he puzzled learned theologians; in manhood he confounded the skeptics; and in his death and resurrection he pointed the way to the meaning of the universe and to personal wholeness.

He has never written a book, yet his life has inspired more books than any other man.

He never wrote a song, yet he has been the theme of more songs than all the songwriters combined in history.

He never founded a university, but all the schools and colleges and universities put together cannot boast of having more students than those following this one man.

He never marshalled an army, drafted a soldier or fired a gun; yet no leader has conquered more people without firing a single shot than this one man.

He did not practise psychiatry, yet he has healed more broken hearts than all the doctors and psychologists the world has known.

The names of great statesmen have come and gone; scientists, philosophers and theologians are generally forgotten. But the name of this man stands out above all others.

Every week hundreds of millions of people gather together, not only to remember him, but to worship his as the Lord of history. The wheels of commerce grind to a halt, and the assemblies of politicians cease their arguing— so that multitudes of his disciples can celebrate this one man.

This man, more than any other, stands on the highest pinnacle of history. He is proclaimed by the lips of more people than any other. He is acknowledged by angels, adored by his followers, and feared by the demons of hell.

Who is he? He is God come to earth. A savior of mankind. He is Jesus Christ.

If you had asked Buddha if *he* deserved such worship, he would have responded, "My son, you are suffering behind the veil of illusion." If you had enquired of Socrates if *he* deserved the worship of multitudes of humanity, he would have mocked and laughed you out of his presence. If you had offered such worship to Muhammad, he would have rent his clothes—and then cut off your head. If you had suggested to Confucius that *he* was the central figure of history, he would have responded that such remarks are in bad taste.

Only Jesus Christ claimed unique deity for himself. Jesus claimed to be God. He didn't leave any other option open. His claim must be either true or false. Jesus asked of his disciples many years ago, "Who do you say that I am?"

And it is a question that everyone must answer. The Bible says that whoever believes in Jesus Christ as the Son of God, and receives him into their heart, has the power to become a child of God.

Who do you think Christ is? What is your answer?

It was Dr Karl Gustav Jung who said, "The central neurosis of our time is emptiness." Sooner or later, if you keep telling people that they are the product of chance, they are going to feel like it. Multitudes of people have been fed the great lie that there is no God. And the result is an ache in the heart of man, a loneliness at the very center of his being, an emptiness that cries out to be filled.

It was Mahatma Ghandi who said, speaking of Jesus, "It is an unbroken torture to me that I am still so far from him, who as I fully know, governs every breath of my life, and whose offspring I am. I know that it is the evil passions within that keep me so far from him, and yet I cannot get away from them." Modern man suffers from more than emptiness, but as Ghandi said, there is also an evil within us that separates us from a loving and holy God.

It is Jesus who came to bridge that great chasm. Religion is man's way of searching for God, but Jesus is God's way of searching for man.

We no longer have to live "lives of quiet desperation". We can go to the One who created us. Jesus came to heal broken hearts, to set people free from their self-made prisons, and to open the eyes of those who want to see the true nature of things.

We were created to be loved. We long to belong. We want to be wanted. God never intended us to hear, "You're no son of mine, no son of mine . . ." Every one of us searches, each of us longs for the love that we were created for.

We were created for friendship. We are not the product of time plus chance plus matter. My friend, you are more significant than that. You were created for a purpose. Your life has a destiny. And that's what this book is all about.

1

Knowing God

PURSUING FRIENDSHIP WITH GOD is the highest calling of every human being. Some people think the study of anthropology is the highest pursuit of knowledge, but they are mistaken. The pursuit of God is the highest science, the greatest philosophy, the most majestic poetry, to which any of us can devote ourselves. God is so vast that all our thoughts are swallowed up in his greatness. He is so deep that no one can fathom him.

We can grapple with other subjects and, when we have mastered them, find a sense of contentment in our achievement. But no one can ever master God. There is no sonar that can plumb his depths, no telescope that can scan his furthest bounds, no microscope that can penetrate his inner being. God's greatness humbles our minds and, at the same time, expands our imaginations. The person who pursues friendship with God will never again be satisfied to simply tread the earth and live out a meaningless existence.

The pursuit of God not only humbles our minds, it humbles our hearts as well. Knowledge of God is *moral* knowledge. It has to do with the purpose of our existence and with *how* our lives are to be lived. When the creature stands before the Creator and comes to know him, a person can only bow down in humble reverence. Are you prepared to submit to God, in greater measure as you know him in greater depth?

The pursuit of God also brings consolation to the soul. In coming to know the greatness of God, a tremendous comfort comes to us. Nothing so brings peace to our spirits when we are troubled, nothing so brings solace to our souls when we are grieved, nothing so brings clarity to our minds when we are confused, as the knowledge of God himself.

If we are to know God as our friend, we must know *God*. We are not intent on becoming friends with a concept or with a theological abstraction; we are interested in becoming friends with a *person*. Friendship is ultimately built on the character of the persons involved. Therefore we must get to know God's nature, God's character, if we are to fully enter into relationship with him.

NO LIMITS

Who is this God who has offered himself in friendship to us?

God is self-existent, infinite, and eternal;
   unchanging,
       almighty,
              and omniscient.
He is God!
  There are
        no limits
           to his greatness!
He is an ever-present God;
   loving,
       merciful,
           and truthful.
Our God is faithful,
   just,
       and holy....

… and the list goes on and on. We could find innumerable ways to describe him, for the reality of God is utterly beyond our ability to capture in words.

A caution before we go any farther: our pursuit of understanding about God is never an end in itself. It is always a means to an end: the goal of knowing *about* God is to *know* God.

Theology can become a form of idolatry for some people. They become so impressed with their knowledge, they forget that the first calling of humankind is to know God personally. Paul warns that "'Knowledge' puffs up, but love builds up" (1 Cor 8:1).

Our goal is not simply to amass knowledge *about* God, ending up in a state of self-satisfied delusion. Our goal is to know God himself, to become friends with him, to enjoy the intimacy he makes available to us… and then to make him known. What greater goal could one ask for in life than to know God and to make him known?!

As we have already noted, we can never learn everything there is to know about God—at least, not in this earthly life. But the very fact that we can never know everything about God is precisely what makes a relationship with him so satisfying. I would find no satisfaction in a relationship with a "finite God" because he could be so quickly and easily comprehended.

But in the God of the Bible we discover a total richness of character and depth of personality that we can continually explore and never exhaust. God is profound beyond our understanding. As Thomas F. Torrance has explained:

God is present to us and gives himself to our knowing only in such a way that he remains the Lord who has ascendancy over us, who distinguishes himself from us and makes himself known in his divine other-ness even when he draws us into communion with himself. He is present to us in such a way that he never resigns knowledge of himself to our mastery.

Hence we can never give account of our knowledge of God in such a way as to reduce his holiness, his transcendency, his unapproachable majesty, to a vanishing point, but only in such a way that we are thrown ultimately upon his mercy, upon his transcendent freedom to lower himself to us and lift us up to him beyond anything we can think or conceive of ourselves.[1]

At the same time, however, our relationship with God is only possible because there *are* some things about him that we *do* understand. We could never have a relationship with any being who was utterly unknown and unknowable. There must be some level of understanding that forms the basis for friendship. We must strive to understand as much as we can about God, even as we recognize that we can never know it all.

In the rest of this chapter, we will consider a few of the characteristics of God: how they are presented in the Bible, the way godly teachers of his Word have helped us understand them, and the way they influence our ability to have relationship with God.

GOD IS INFINITE

Am I a God at hand, says the LORD, and not a God afar off? Can a man hide himself in secret places so that I cannot see him? says the LORD. Do I not fill heaven and earth? says the LORD.   Jer 23:23-24

But will God indeed dwell on the earth? Behold, heaven and the highest heaven cannot contain thee!   1 Kgs 8:27

To say that God is infinite is to say that he is unbounded, unconfined. He is not bound by any of the constraints that affect you and me, such as space, distance, or size. In every conceivable way (and doubtless in some ways of which we humans cannot conceive!) God is immeasurable.

It is the very fact that he is infinite, while we are finite, that places God so far beyond our comprehension. The more we understand about him, the more we realize how much there is about him that we do not understand. The better we get to know him, the more we realize how much more there is for us to get to know.

This is one of the reasons why God has always forbidden his people to make *idols* or "vain images" of his likeness. People who believe in any deity are prone to the worship of idols for one simple reason: they long to see and touch the God they believe in. Such a longing is a natural expression of our finite nature, wanting to "get a handle on" the infinite.

But God knows that any attempt we might make to represent him by the work of our hands is bound to *mis*represent him. Any likeness we make is certain to be a reflection of *our limited conception* of God, not of God as he actually is. It amounts to humankind creating God in our own image and likeness, rather than the other way around. God's prohibition against "graven images" helps us remember that he is infinite—and infinitely beyond our ability to contain or control him.

The scriptural images of God's infinity often concern a particular trait that the theologians call his *immensity* or his *omnipresence*. For example, we speak of God "being everywhere at once." This doesn't mean that his toes stretch over Alaska and his nose hovers over Paris, but that the fullness of God fills all things. The Creator of all transcends all our earth-bound notions of space and location.

We are also accustomed to speaking of God as *eternal*,

referring to the fact that he also transcends the boundaries of time. You and I are always "hemmed in" by time. Our very existence is defined by the clock and the calendar. We have a beginning and an end. Not so with God. He has no beginning, and no end. It is simply impossible to describe or define him in terms of the clock or the calendar.

That doesn't mean that God cannot step into our time frame and relate to us on those terms. He can, and he does: the whole Bible is an account of his doing precisely that. God is intimately involved in the human drama—not just as a member of the audience, not even as a member of the cast, but as a sort of combination playwright/ actor/ director who brings the whole play into being and who interactively participates with the players onstage. The infinite God steps into the finite realm that he has created, and his actions then become measureable in time.

Although God is not hemmed in by time, he does act sequentially, one action after the other. "In the beginning, God…" God is himself *outside time*, but he interacts with humankind *within time* as we know it and he created it to be. When the Bible says in Jeremiah 18:7-10 that he will not judge a nation if they turn to him, he means exactly what he says:

> If at any time I declare concerning a nation or a kingdom, that I will pluck up and break down and destroy it, and if that nation, concerning which I have spoken, turns from its evil, I will repent of the evil that I intended to do to it. And if at any time I declare concerning a nation or a kingdom that I will build and plant it, and if it does evil in my sight, not listening to my voice, then I will repent of the good which I had intended to do to it.

Prayer and intercession are God's way of allowing us to participate with him in truly influencing individuals and entire nations. God listens when people respond to him, and he responds in turn according to our actions and choices.

The only limitations on God's infiniteness are those that he places on himself in allowing us to exercise our free will. We can thwart the plans of God. We can turn away from his marvelous grace. This grieves God, but it does not detract from his greatness or power or knowledge.

God has chosen to allow our choices to affect him. How awesome that he gives humankind this measure of freedom—and responsibility. God's plan for our lives is not static, like a computer printout. He is dynamic, creative, constantly acting and creating new possibilities and plans in response to our obedience or disobedience.

The above statement from Jeremiah 18:7-10 about God's willingness to respond to Israel's choices is not just the prophet's attempt to say something about God in human terms, but is truly how he relates to us. Our choices, our prayers, really do make a difference to him.

Who can comprehend an infinite God who interacts with finite beings in such a loving manner? *No one.* No theologian is capable of explaining God, no human being can contain him. He is God!

When God does break into our finite existence and reveal something about himself, what he reveals is authentic and true. He doesn't just make up a story for us to believe in, but he shows us something of himself *as he really is.* So our knowledge of God is true, albeit not exhaustive. We can grasp it, but we can never *completely* understand it. When we reach the boundary of what we are able to understand, the most appropriate response is then to fall down on our knees in worship.

GOD IS SELF-EXISTENT

Then Moses said to God, "If I come to the people of Israel and say to them, 'The God of your fathers has sent me to you,' and they ask me, 'What is his name?' what shall I say to them?" God said to Moses, "I AM WHO I AM." And he said, "Say this to the people of Israel, "I AM has sent me to you" (Ex 3:13-14).

> For as the Father has life in himself, so he has granted the Son also to have life in himself.... Jn 5:26

The moment we begin to speak of God as eternal, as having no beginning and no end, we bring up the question that all of us asked when we were children. You remember how it went. The child asks, "Who made me, Daddy?" The father (or mother or Sunday School teacher) answers, "God made you." The child then raises the obvious next question: "And who made God?" To the mind of a youngster, the answer to that question is usually unsatisfying and confusing: "No one made God; he just *is*."

Most adults still puzzle over it! Of all the characteristics of God, this is perhaps the hardest one for us to grasp. God is the only being we know who has this quality. We ourselves have no experience of it whatsoever—nothing we can relate it to, nothing of which we can say, "Well, it's sort of like...."

I suspect that Moses may have been similarly confused at the answer God gave *him*. Moses had asked what seemed like a perfectly reasonable question: "What's your name?" And God answered him with one of the most profound and impenetrable statements imaginable: "I AM." His very name calls attention to this basic attribute of his nature: his self-existence.

One of the things that you and I do have in common with God is that we both exist. The difference is that you and I have *received* our existence from him. If God had not created us, we would not *be*; if he had not given us the gift of existence, we would not exist. But no one created God. No one *gave* him the gift of existence. The gift of being, of existence, resides in himself. This is what Jesus meant when he said that the Father "has life in himself." God was not created. He did not "come into being." God just *is*.

Beyond that, we must simply accept the principle of God's self-existence as a starting point for our worship, as one of the characteristics of God before which we can only stand in awe. We can also be grateful that God chose to share the gift of being with us so that we can enjoy intimate friendship with him.

GOD IS ALL-POWERFUL

"Behold, I am the LORD, the God of all flesh; is anything too hard for me?" Jer 32:27

And Jesus came and said to them, "All authority in heaven and on earth has been given to me." Mt 28:18

From the beginning of the Bible to the end, we see God demonstrating his omnipotence. He reveals his power in the creation of the universe: God spoke and everything came into being. That same power sustains the universe, as Paul wrote in his letter to the Colossians concerning Jesus:

... in him all things were created, in heaven and on earth, visible or invisible, whether thrones or dominions or principalities or authorities—all things were created through him and for him. He is before all things, and *in him all things hold together*. Col 1:16-17, emphasis mine

The same power that created the universe raised Lazarus from the dead: Jesus spoke, and Lazarus came out of the tomb (see Jn 11:1-44). That same power raised Jesus from the dead. The same power that created the universe and raised Jesus from the dead is also active in our lives right now. Paul prayed that the Ephesians would come to know "the immeasurable greatness of his power in us who believe, according to the working of his great might which he accomplished in Christ when he raised him from the dead" (Eph 1:19-20).

To the very end, the Scriptures stress God's power. In the book of Revelation we read: "'I am the Alpha and the Omega,' says the Lord God, who is and who was and who is to come, the Almighty" (Rv 1:8).

God's omnipotence can seem contradictory to the concept of free will. Who among us hasn't heard the old conundrum, "If God is almighty, can he create a rock so big that he himself cannot lift it?" The only response, of course, is that it is not a question at all but a piece of nonsense. As C.S. Lewis once wrote, "Omnipotence means power to do all that is intrinsically possible but not to do the intrinsically impossible. You may attribute miracles to [God], but not nonsense."[2]

Don't you find it a bit frightening to be in relationship with an almighty being—one who has no limit, except that which he imposes on himself, on his ability to do whatever he chooses? But we must remember that God's power is always subject to his goodness. He does not use his power to dominate us or to crush us; he does not use his power capriciously or for selfish purposes. Rather God uses it always and only for *our* good. As Mary proclaimed in her majestic prayer, the Magnificat, "he who is mighty has done great things for me, and holy is his name" (Lk 1:49). He is not a God of force, but one whose power is always used in conformity to his own laws, and in the service of his love.

GOD IS SPIRIT

Whither shall I go from thy Spirit?
    Or whither shall I flee from thy presence?
If I ascend up into heaven, thou art there!

If I make my bed in Sheol, thou art there!
If I take the wings of the morning
    and dwell in the uttermost parts of the sea,
even there thy hand shall lead me
    and thy right hand shall hold me.   Ps 139:7-10

"God is spirit, and those who worship him must worship in spirit and truth."   Jn 4:24

A speaker was once trying to explain to a skeptical audience what "spirit" was like. He described it as having "no height, no depth, no weight, no color, no size, and no shape."

"That," replied a man in the crowd, "is the most perfect definition of 'nothing' I've ever heard."

It may seem that way to us, too. But God is most definitely not "nothing." He is "something." The problem is that this particular "something" happens to be entirely outside our personal experience. Our bodies are composed of matter, of something that *does* have height and depth and weight and all the rest. God is not like that. He is spirit, although nonetheless very personal at the same time.

Most of the concepts we normally try to associate with "spirit" are unhelpful. For example, we might picture spirit as a sort of gaseous cloud or vapor. But of course gases and vapors are also matter, as you may recall from high school science class. They are just matter in a different form.

Or we might picture spirit as the notorious "force" of *Star Wars* fame. Wrong again. God can *produce* force, but spirit and force are different things. Force is impersonal, but spirit is intensely personal. God is not just some*thing*, but some*one*. Spirit can feel and think and choose.

How can we have relationship with a God who is spirit? For one thing, we can have relationship with God because he has taken on humanity—taken on a body made of matter—and come to us in the person of Jesus. For another, we can have relationship with him because his Spirit comes to dwell within us.

A moment ago I said that "spirit" was entirely outside our personal experience. Perhaps I should have said, "outside our *conscious* personal experience." Even though we may not be aware of it, human beings are also partially spirit. In our case, we are talking about a finite spirit inhabiting a material body.

In God's case, we are talking about an infinite spirit that is not bound by a material body. Because Jesus came to us a man, we are able to relate to God on the material level. Because we ourselves are part spirit, we are able to relate to him on the spiritual level as well.

GOD IS TRUTH

I the LORD speak the truth,
I declare what is right.   Is 45:19

"For this I was born, for this I have come into the world, to bear witness to the truth. Everyone who is of the truth hears my voice."   Jn 18:37

"I am the way, and the truth, and the life."   Jn 14:6

We may not think about how helpful it is to know that God is truthful—that he never lies to us, never misleads us, never "tricks" or "fools" us. We tend to take it for granted that God is honest, that he plays straight with us.

But consider for a moment what it would be like to have a God who was *not* honest, who could not be counted on to be real with us. But in fact God is utterly truthful. In him there is no error. His word is true, his actions are true, his character is true, his law is true.

My point is not merely that God *tells* the truth, but that God *is* truth. He is the complete and perfect expression of truth. All truth resides in him. Apart from God, there *is* no truth: the very concept is meaningless apart from him.

Three aspects to biblical truth are important for us to understand, especially in regard to finding and building an ever deepening friendship with God. The first is that truth is *objective, not subjective.* Quite often, when I have told someone of my faith in Jesus, they will respond by saying, "Well, all that is true for *you*, because you believe it. But I don't believe it, so it's not true for *me*."

I then say, "Wait a minute. You don't understand what I'm saying. I'm not saying that I have merely conjured up a mental concept called 'God' that exists only so long as I hold it in my mind. I am saying there is a God who exists in the same way that Mount Everest or the city of London exists. In a radically different way, God is *there*—apart from you and me, outside the realm of anyone's imagination. He would exist whether I believed in him or not. And he exists whether *you* believe in him or not!"

The second aspect of truth is that it is *personal and concrete, not impersonal and abstract.* We are called not just to say yes to a concept or to a philosophical ideal, but to follow a person. Jesus did not say, "I *know* the truth." He said, "I *am* the truth." He is the embodiment, the very incarnation, of truth. By the same token, if we are to enjoy relationship with God, the truth must become incarnate in our lives. We must not simply believe the truth, we must *live* the truth.

This suggests the third aspect of truth: that it is a *verb, not a noun.* It is not just something to be known, but something to be done. James cautions us that truth bears a "use it or lose it" quality:

Be doers of the word, and not hearers only, deceiving yourselves. For if any one is a hearer of the word and not a doer, he is like a man who observes his natural face in a mirror; for he observes himself and goes away and at once forgets what he was like. But he who looks into the perfect law, the law of liberty, and perseveres, being no hearer that forgets but a doer that acts, he shall be blessed in his doing.

Jas 1:22-25

GOD IS UNCHANGING

"For I the LORD do not change...." Mal 3:6

Every good endowment and every perfect gift is from above, coming down from the Father of lights with whom there is no variation or shadow due to change. Jas 1:17

Jesus Christ is the same yesterday and today and for ever.

Heb 13:8

The theologians refer to this characteristic as the *immutability* of God. It has to do with God's constancy, his consistency, his reliability. His nature, his character, never changes.

This does not mean that God is inert or static—that he "just sits there" like a lump of coal. God is alive, active, still creating, still re-creating, still redeeming, still responding to the prayers of his people—but always within the context of his never-changing nature.

Have you ever puzzled over those instances in the Bible when God seems to "change his mind," when he first threatens to destroy someone because of his sin, and then spares him instead—either because of the person's own repentance or because of someone else's intercession? Rather than fickleness, these stories demonstrate the unchanging *mercy* of God. They tell us that because God is the way he is, it is never too late for us to turn back to him and receive his forgiveness, rather than the punishment we deserve.

We could speak of the immutability of God with regard to a number of particular aspects of his character:

- God's *eternal being* does not change. "Of old thou didst lay the foundation of the earth,/ and the heavens are the work of thy hands./ They will perish, but thou dost endure;/ they will all wear out like a garment./ Thou changest them like a raiment, and they pass away;/ but thou art the same, and thy years have no end" (Ps 102:25-27).

- God's *character* does not change. A human being's character can be impacted by stress, hardship, or changing circumstances, but God always remains the same. "For I the LORD do not change..." (Mal 3:6).

- God's *truth* does not change. "The grass withers, the flower fades;/ but the word of our God will stand for ever" (Is 40:8).

- God's *ways* do not change. "And also the Glory of Israel will not lie or repent; for he is not a man, that he should repent" (1 Sm 15:29).

- God's *Son* does not change. "Jesus Christ is the same yesterday and today and forever" (Heb 13:8).

Many things in life change: people, work, friendship, family. Life on this earth has a transitory nature to it. People come and go in our lives. We may move from one place to another, or switch jobs often. We learn to protect ourselves from these changes, to erect walls that keep others from hurting us. We try to build stability and safety into our lives in the midst of this rapid-fire flux.

But one thing never changes, and that is God. He is always there, faithful, true, available, committed to us. We can count on God. He is the one sure thing in our constantly shifting lives, the still point in a turning world. He is the foundation of our existence, the rock upon which we stand.

GOD IS MAJESTIC

> The LORD reigns; he is robed in majesty....
>> thy throne is established from of old....   Ps 93:1-2

> For the LORD is a great God,
>> and a great king above all gods....
> O come, let us worship and bow down,
>> let us kneel before the LORD, our maker!   Ps 95:3, 6

This quality goes by a variety of different names: the greatness of God, the glory of God, the awesomeness of God, to name only a few. Essentially, it is that characteristic of God which causes something deep inside us to stand in awe of God. The one that prompts us to fall down and worship him, the way a subject would kneel before his king. That, in fact, is precisely our situation: we are subjects bowing down to the King of the universe.

A friend of mine once said that everyone, whether they know it or not, is living for *something*. Human beings naturally give themselves over to that which they consider most deserving of their time and money and attention. They will sacrifice and struggle for it, even lay down their lives for it... and when they are finished, say that it was well worth it all.

God is the one who most deserves our devotion. The book of Revelation describes the entire population of heaven bowing before him, crying out, "Worthy art thou, our Lord and God, to receive glory and honor and power, for thou didst create all things, and by thy will they existed and were created" (Rv 4:11). As we grow in relationship with him, we come more and more to recognize his worthiness, his greatness, his majesty—and our hearts respond accordingly.

As we begin to glimpse God's awesome majesty, we also realize more and more clearly how inappropriate it is to let other things compete with him for first place in our lives. The saints of old said that the best of created things can disappoint us and even torment us.

Perhaps you've seen the bumper sticker that says, "The one who dies with the most toys, wins." But after we have played with our toys and pushed our buttons and been entertained by our gadgets, do we not realize that only God can satisfy our souls? How much money do we have to spend, how much time do we need to give, how much energy do we need to expend, before we allow this majestic God to capture our hearts—before we accept his offer of friendship and restful abiding?

GOD IS WISE

> he gives wisdom to the wise
>   and knowledge to the those who have understanding;
> he reveals deep and mysterious things;
>   he knows what is in the darkness,
>   and the light dwells with him.   Dn 2:21-22

> If any of you lacks wisdom, let him ask God, who gives to all men generously and without reproaching, and it will be given him.   Jas 1:5

It is one thing, of course, to say that God himself is wise. That, after all, is what we would expect; wisdom is in keeping with everything else we have learned about him. But the really good news is that God makes his wisdom available to *us*. Indeed, his wisdom never fails us. It is always available to us for the asking.

I am not claiming that this all-wise God will deliver us from all the problems created by ourselves and others. Our heavenly Father does not impose a trouble-free life on us, but he does intend a life that will lead us into fellowship with him, a life that will help us grow into holiness, a life that will serve as a witness to others about him. Severe troubles often provide the most profound opportunities.

Consider the example of Joseph, whose rejection and exile provided the opportunity to rescue his family from famine. Joseph relied upon the wisdom of God in interpreting dreams and advising Pharaoh. We also see Daniel giving counsel to kings, standing firm on God's wisdom, and being rescued from the mouth of the lion.

In our time we see people like Corrie Ten Boom, arrested by the Nazis and thrown into a concentration camp, being led by God's wisdom in how not only to survive but also to help others. Or Joni Eareckson, confined to a wheelchair as the result of a tragic accident, receiving God's wisdom for coping with her situation and for being a blessing to others.

Such is the Father's promise: that in every difficult circumstance, in every trying situation, in every perplexing problem, he has an answer for us. We have only to seek God's wisdom as to how the various aspects of his character—his righteousness, his mercy, his justice—can shine through our own lives.

Every direction God gives us is backed up by his infinite wisdom. Many Christians are afraid that if they totally surrender their lives to his control, God will ask them to go someplace or do something difficult, to give up friends, or family, or comforts, to serve as a missionary in "darkest Africa" or as a pastor in the "urban jungle."

Their mistake is that they are focusing more on what God may ask them to do, than on *who* is speaking to them. Would an all wise, loving, holy, truthful, faithful God ask us to do something or go someplace that is not wise, loving, and holy? Obviously not. Rather, God helps us to recognize the wisest choice or action at that very moment, and then gives us the grace to choose it.

Study God's character, get to know him in the Bible and through Jesus as the always loving, infinitely wise God that he

is… and you will not question his goodness or his ability to
guide and govern your life.

GOD IS HOLY

> You shall be holy to me; for I the LORD am holy, and have
> separated you from the peoples, that you should be mine.
>
> **Lv 20:26**

> Holy, holy, holy is the LORD of hosts; the whole earth is full
> of his glory. Is 6:3

> Who shall not fear and glorify thy name, O Lord? For thou
> alone art holy. Rv 15:4

The essence of holiness is separateness. When we say that
God is holy, we mean that he is exalted above all his creatures,
and that he is wholly separate from moral evil. The Bible tells
us in every imaginable way that God is perfect in purity:

- God the Father is holy (Jn 17:11).
- God the Son is holy (Mt 1:8).
- God the Spirit is holy (Mk 1:8).
- God's name is holy (Ex 27).
- God is to be worshiped in holiness (Ps 22:3).
- There is wisdom in God's holiness (Prv 9:10).
- There is power in God's holiness (Ps 99:3-5).
- There is joy in God's holiness (Rom 14:7).
- God redeems in holiness (Is 41:20).
- God judges in holiness (Is 5:16).

The obvious ramification of this holiness, this separateness,
is the cavernous chasm between God and humankind. We
cannot bridge this gulf unless God makes it possible. We cannot overcome this difference unless God makes us like himself—or makes himself like us. And that, of course, is exactly

what God offers to do through his Son Jesus. It is possible to have friendship with the Holy One because God has bridged the chasm, has freed us from our bondage to sin, and has come to dwell within us through the Holy Spirit.

GOD IS LOVE

> Beloved, let us love one another; for love is of God, and he who loves is born of God and knows God. He who does not love does not know God; for God is love. 1 Jn 4:7-8

Love is the ultimate truth about God, the characteristic that sums up everything else and draws together all the aspects of his nature. God loves us. Think about that for a moment: *God loves us.* The poets are right when they say that it is a wonderful thing to be loved by someone. And surely the most wonderful thing of all is to be loved by God himself.

While this overwhelming truth could be discussed without end, let's focus here on four aspects of God's love that pertain especially to our enjoying intimacy with him.

First, love is God's most basic *motivation* for seeking relationship with us. It was out of the overwhelming generosity and goodness of his heart that God created us. After we turned from him, love moved him to redeem us so that we could be restored to friendship with him.

Second, love flows out of *who God is.* Love is not just an occasional emotion for God, not just something he does every once in a while. Love is who God *is.*

Third, God is *faithful* to those he loves. He has committed himself to be loyal to us no matter what. He has pledged to love us whether we love him in return or not. This is what the Bible calls a "covenant," a promise offered to us by God.

Fourth, God's love is *unconditional.* God never stops loving us, no matter what we do. His love is the rock-bottom reality upon which everything else in our lives can be based. Even though we may fail him and suffer the consequences of our disobedience, God still loves us. In fact, it is his love for us that causes our heavenly Father to grieve when we reject him or disobey him.

The Bible teaches that a person's sin will eventually separate him from God for eternity if he does not repent and turn his life over to God. That humankind suffers the consequences of rebellion against God does not mean he does not love us. Scripture says, "For God sent the Son into the world, not to condemn the world, but that the world might be saved through him.... This is the judgment, that the light has come into the world, and men loved darkness rather than light, because their deeds were evil" (Jn 3:17-19).

I know it is a bit overwhelming to contemplate so many different facets of God's nature so rapidly. And these are but a few of God's countless qualities and attributes! No one understands God perfectly—and our ability to be friends with God in no way depends on our mastery of theology. There is no "entrance exam" that we must pass before God will come to us and extend his offer of friendship to us.

But isn't it only natural that if you love someone you will want to get to know them better? Of course, God already knows everything there is to know about each of us. And he is only too glad to make himself known to us as we seek after him in purity and simplicity of heart. By coming to earth in the person of Jesus, God gave us a sort of "ultimate audio-visual aid" as to what he is like. We draw closer to God by drawing closer to his Son. It is him to whom we now turn our attention.

2

What a Friend We Have in Jesus

JOSEPH SCRIVEN WAS ILL.

Born in Dublin in 1820, Scriven had studied for the Anglican ministry at Trinity College and gone on to a long career as a pastor. His life had been marked by tragedy. As a young man, he was engaged to be married. But on the day before the wedding was to have occurred, his bride-to-be drowned in an accident. Scriven left England to get away from the terrible memories, eventually settling down in Canada. Now he was sick, perhaps near death.

A neighbor was sitting by Scriven's sickbed, keeping him company, caring for his needs, consoling him. The neighbor happened to notice a sheet of paper with some words on it, tucked underneath Scriven's Bible on the nightstand. "What's this?" he asked.

It was a song—a hymn, actually. Scriven and a friend had written it years before, when Scriven's mother was going through a prolonged illness. He had wanted to comfort her with some of the spiritual insight he had gained from the death of his fiancée. He had not intended for the hymn to be seen by anyone else, let alone to be published. The words struck Scriven's friend as profound:

What a friend we have in Jesus,
  All our sins and griefs to bear;
What a privilege to carry
  Everything to God in prayer.

O, what peace we often forfeit!
  O what needless pain we bear!
All because we do not carry
  everything to God in prayer.

Can we find a friend so faithful,
  who will all our sorrows share?
Jesus knows our every weakness;
  Take it to the Lord in prayer.[1]

When the famous evangelist Dwight L. Moody heard Scriven's hymn, he was so touched that he began using it in his evangelistic crusades. Today "What a Friend We Have in Jesus" remains one of the best-loved of all hymns.

I once asked a friend why she thought so many people failed to understand the friendship God offers them, why they did not enjoy it and live it and thrive in it. She pointed to two passages in Paul's letter to the Ephesians that she thought held the answer.

In the first passage, Paul prays "that the God of our Lord Jesus Christ, the Father of glory, may give you a spirit of wisdom and of revelation in the knowledge of him, *having the eyes of your hearts enlightened, that you may know what is the hope to which he has called you, what are the riches of his glorious inheritance in the saints, and what is the immeasurable greatness of his power in us who believe"* (Eph 1:17-19, italics mine).

Later in the letter, Paul again prays fervently, "that you, being rooted and grounded in love, may have power to comprehend with all the saints what is the breadth and length and height and depth, and to know the love of Christ which surpasses knowledge, that you may be filled with all the fulness of God" (Eph 3:17-19).

Do you see the common thread in these two prayers? In both cases, Paul is acknowledging that God has made known to us all that we need to grasp his outstretched hand of friendship... but that we come against a spiritual battle in *comprehending* that revelation. It's as though we have a mental sieve in place that only lets the liquid pass through, but stops the larger bits of God's truth from passing through to reach our hearts.

Thus Paul prays that "the eyes of our hearts may be open" to see what God is offering us, that we may have the "power to comprehend" it. When that happens—and *only* when that happens—will we see that we don't have to strive or strain or achieve or perform in order to earn God's love. We can accept his offer of friendship and enjoy intimacy with Jesus.

WHO IS THIS JESUS?

What are some of the things God wants us to see and understand about his only Son? As in the last chapter, we could compile a list that would be virtually endless. But let's briefly consider a few key characteristics of who Jesus is. As the Holy Spirit answers Paul's prayer by helping us comprehend them, these bits of truth will sink deeper into our hearts and strengthen our relationship with him.

First, Jesus is the Creator and sustainer of the universe. Usually we attribute these functions to God the Father, and rightly so. But the Bible says that Jesus was God's *agent* in

creating and sustaining the universe. As Paul says, "He is...
the first-born of all creation; for in him all things were created, in heaven and on earth, visible and invisible... all things
were created through him and for him. He is before all
things, and in him all things hold together" (Col 1:15-17).

Second, Jesus is God in human form. As I mentioned
before, Jesus is a sort of ultimate audio-visual aid as to what
God is like, "the image of the invisible God... in him all the
fulness of God was pleased to dwell" (Col 1:15, 19). As Jesus
himself told his disciples, "He who has seen me has seen the
Father" (Jn 14:9).

Third, Jesus is the Savior of the world. His alone is the
blood that redeems men and women from bondage to evil.
His alone is the body that was broken for our healing. His
alone is the sacrifice that atones for our sins. "And there is salvation in no one else, for there is no other name under
heaven given among men by which we must be saved" (Acts
4:12).

Fourth, Jesus is the Shepherd of the church. He is not
only the Lamb whose sacrifice saved us, but also the Shepherd
who leads us, guides us, and protects us. He alone has the
right to rule over the church he bought with his blood. He is
the church's one foundation and its master builder. "He is the
head of the body, the church" (Col 1:18).

Fifth, Jesus is the sovereign Lord of the universe. Because
he *is* the source of creation, because he *is* the image of God,
because he *is* the Savior, and because he *is* the church's chief
Shepherd, Jesus is also absolute ruler over all.

It is before Jesus that every person must appear at the end
of time for the judgment of their sins. It is by him that every

person will be measured. Jesus is the measuring rod of holiness. It is unto him that every being will ultimately bow the knee, and of him that every tongue will ultimately confess, "Jesus Christ is Lord, to the glory of God the Father" (Phil 2:11).

DEEPER AND DEEPER

Some Christians seem to enjoy a greater closeness, a deeper intimacy with Jesus than others. They develop what I call a "reverent familiarity" that seems almost foreign to the rest of us. What's the reason for this? Is it favoritism on God's part? Are these people especially mystical, or perhaps overly presumptuous? Are they simply experiencing some kind of emotional high and *calling* it a spiritual relationship?

No. As with any personal relationship, there really are degrees of intimacy with God. But it is we, not God, who determine the degree of intimacy we will enjoy with him. Let me say that again, because it is such a radical idea for many of us: *The degree of intimacy we have with God is up to us.* We can be as close to him as *we want to be.*

Since God loves us unconditionally, we can do nothing to earn or deserve his love. He offers his friendship to us as a free gift. But God does place *conditions* upon our relationship, certain boundaries that affect our ability to receive and experience his love. Just as in a marriage, there is a price to be paid for intimacy.

If we are not experiencing everything we would like in our relationship with God, it could be because we simply don't know what is available to us. A failure to understand friendship with God is precisely the problem this book aims to solve. It could be because certain obstacles stand between us and God, (as discussed in chapter five).

It could be that we have not chosen to draw closer to him. If so, it is we who are the losers. God will not force himself on us. But he always stands ready to respond to us as we open ourselves to him.

I said a moment ago that there are degrees of intimacy with God. Let me explain what I mean—with the goal of setting out a sort of road map that you can follow in drawing closer to the Lord. Wherever you may be along the way, remember: you can always go farther, deeper into God.

First, we can know Jesus as our Savior, as the one who has saved us from our sin. The apostle John said, "My little children, I am writing this to you, so that you may not sin... (1 Jn 2:1). This is the starting point for all of us.

It was the beginning for Annemarie, a woman we knew in Amsterdam. Annemarie had been a prostitute for twenty-one years—all her adult life. She worked the street just outside the Cleft, the name of our headquarters in the red-light district.

Two of our workers, Warren and Marietha, felt a special burden for Annemarie. Every day they would seek her out and invite her to come inside our outreach center. "You know, Jesus loves you, Annemarie," they would say. "Why don't you come over to the Cleft and let us help you? Maybe fix you a meal? Give you a place to stay for a while?" They never tried to cram religion down her throat, just persistently offered to help her.

This went on for four years—almost every day of the week. Warren and Marietha would invite Annemarie in, and always she would say no. She was emotionally calloused, afraid to show need or weakness to anyone.

Then one day, for some reason, Annemarie gave in... just a little. Warren invited her in for a meal. Even though she hadn't eaten in a couple days and was desperately hungry, she still said no. Then Marietha went out and pleaded with her a second time, and this time she said yes. Annemarie came into the Cleft for supper.

As Warren and Marietha bowed their heads to say grace, something touched this woman deep in the recesses of her heart. After dinner she stayed for the evening Bible study and listened with rapt attention. And when it was over, Annemarie gave her life to Jesus. She had met the Savior.

That was six years ago, and Annemarie has never been the same since. For months after her conversion, she came to our Bible studies and prayer meetings and just sat there—weeping for joy, overwhelmed that Jesus had forgiven her. This woman who had labored for twenty-one years as a prostitute was like a dry and thirsty sponge, soaking up the grace and mercy of God.

Not long ago an utterly astonishing thing happened. We knew that years ago Annemarie had given birth to a baby boy, whom she immediately gave up for adoption. Now, completely independent of the transformation in her own life, Annemarie's teenage son had accepted Christ.

The youth decided to seek out his mother. He knew she was a prostitute, and he knew where to look for her: in the red-light district. Imagine his joy when he found her—and learned that she was not only his mother, but also that she too had trusted Christ to be her Savior!

The next stage of intimacy is to know Jesus not only as our Savior but also as our friend. My father is a pastor, what's called a "pioneer preacher" or a "church planter." Back in the early fifties, Dad started a new church in Long Beach, California. It met in a little store on busy Redondo Avenue.

There were some real characters in that church. My dad gave them endearing nicknames. There was Tightwad Malarney, who was so stingy with his money that he wanted everyone to know when he gave a donation. He used to hold his hand a couple feet above the offering plate so the coins would make a loud noise when they landed. There was Garlic Joe. Dad especially liked him because he always sat in the back, which made everyone else move forward to get away from the strong garlic odor on his breath.

And there was Groaning George, whose nickname came from the heart-rending prayers he offered to God. His real name was George Smith, and he was the youth leader of the church. I remember one night, about three in the morning, we suddenly heard a loud knock at our door. There stood George. He had just devoted two solid weeks—his entire vacation—to seeking God in prayer.

George stood on our doorstep and cried, "Pastor Mc-Clung, I need help. God has revealed to me the selfishness of my heart, and I want to know him as more than just my Savior. I desperately need God. *Will you help me?*"

George Smith was willing to pay the price for deeper intimacy with the Lord. And that night, by faith, he opened his life to a whole new level of friendship with God.

I met Jesus as my personal Savior in that very same church on Redondo Avenue. I remember it as clear as a bell. I was nine years old at the time. An itinerant evangelist came through and held a series of meetings. One night I responded to one of his altar calls: I went forward and accepted Jesus. And for many years I lived secure in the knowledge that Christ was my Savior.

I didn't take the next step until several years later. I was in college, studying theology and Greek grammar (and not having much success with the latter, I might add). One day, while my class was struggling through the letter to the Galatians, our professor suddenly stopped. "Do you understand what we're reading?" he said. I looked up. Tears were glistening in his eyes. "We're reading about Jesus and the price he paid so that we could be free from all vestiges of manmade religion, and so that we could know God as our friend."

In that very moment, I realized that even though I had known Jesus all those years, I had been laboring under a religious system. When I had formally joined the church, I was given a rule book telling me all the things I could do and couldn't do and should do and shouldn't do. It seemed that everything in life had a rule connected with it. I found it impossible even to turn around without breaking one of them.

What joy came in my heart, right there in Greek class, to realize that I was saved by God's grace, fully pardoned, fully accepted, and that there was nothing I could do to earn it and nothing I could do to add to it. For years I had known Jesus as my Savior. But that day I came to know him as my friend.

An indispensable stage of any growing relationship with our Lord Jesus is to recognize and accept his right to be the Lord over every aspect of our lives. Whether this is the first stage in a genuine friendship with God or the last is immaterial: it is inevitable.

He is God. He is the creator of the universe and ruler over all that is. He alone is worthy or able to govern our lives. Not to acknowledge or accept him as absolute sovereign over our daily affairs is utter foolishness—or stubborn rebellion.

By surrendering to Jesus as Lord of our lives we are acknowledging our inability to rule our own affairs. Further, we are confessing that the only righteous basis for friendship with God is truth. He is God: holy and wise. Only such a God can guide and govern every dimension of our lives. Not to accept his lordship is to reject truth and no friendship with God can grow without such truth.

The next stage of growth involves becoming co-laborers with God. Another leap forward occurs when we realize that

God not only wants to save us and befriend us but also to make us his partners. We reach a point where we're no longer satisfied just being blessed by God, but we want to bless him and bless others in his name. We want our life to count for the kingdom. We're ready to go anywhere he asks us to go and do anything he asks us to do.

My teenage years seemed pretty ordinary. I went to school and tried my best. I was interested in girls. I was fanatical about basketball. But in the summer of my nineteenth year, I went on a summer outreach trip with Youth with a Mission, and after that I was never satisfied with "ordinary" again.

We were in a place called Bird Rock, on the island of St. Kitt's in the Caribbean. A group of us had walked for hours in the blazing sun to reach a small, distant village. We went from hut to hut trying to find someone who would let us tell them about Jesus. No one would talk to us. No one would so much as let us come in out of the heat!

Finally we met one little old lady who was already a Christian. She was so glad to see us! She invited us in, gave us something cold to drink, and then prayed for us. Before we left, this thoroughly delightful lady asked us to pray for her. We could see that she had a terrible hunchback. "I want to be healed," she said.

We prayed… and prayed… and prayed. The woman herself was very enthusiastic, praising the Lord and praying with us. But nothing happened. Still, we were encouraged by the mere experience of having met her, and walked back to the main city thankful to the Lord.

Three days later, I saw her again. As we were getting ready to leave the city, I heard someone calling my name. It was the same woman, but what a difference! She was standing perfectly upright. "God has healed my back!" she exclaimed.

I was beside myself with joy and gratitude—not just that the Lord had healed her, which was wonderful enough, but that he had chosen to do it *through me*. After that I was hooked. What else in life could compare with being used by God to touch others?

I'm not saying we always need to go around praying for God to heal people, and until he does, we're not his partners. Just the opposite is true: God wants to share *everything* he has made with us. He wants to work through very ordinary folks—just like you and me—to touch other people's lives.

I believe that this desire to bring us into partnership was present in God's heart right from the beginning of creation. I can imagine God saying to himself, "Wouldn't it be fantastic if there were some others who could share in the wonders of my creation?" So he created men and women with mind and intellect and imagination, and said, "Here, I created this world just for you. Live in it. Work with it. Have dominion over it. Here, I will create notes and sounds so that you can produce music. I will create color and shape so that you can produce art. I will give you the raw materials so that you can use the abilities I have given you and share in the joy I feel, the joy of creation."

A RADICAL TRANSFORMATION

In his second letter to the church at Corinth, Paul writes, "And we all, with unveiled face, beholding the glory of the Lord, are being changed into his likeness from one degree of glory to another; for this comes from the Lord who is the Spirit" (2 Cor 3:18).

"Changed into his likeness" is an amazing phrase. Translated in other versions of Scripture as "transformed," it comes from the Greek word for "metamorphosis." Paul is saying we should expect a continuous metamorphosis, a transformation, taking place in each of us. We are changing, from one degree of Christlikeness to another. The degrees may not be readily visible, but the transformation is nonetheless just as real.

Notice also that Paul puts it in the present tense: "are being changed." In Greek grammar, this is what is called the continuous present tense. We could translate it, "we keep on being transformed." The change is not just something that happens once and for all in our lives—or something that is yet to happen in the future. It is happening *now*. And it is happening *continually*, often without our conscious awareness.

Now notice that the phrase is written in the passive voice, rather than the active voice. Paul does not say, "We transform ourselves," or, "we are always seeking to make changes in ourselves." He says, "we *are being* transformed." This process is not something *we do*, but rather something that is *done to us*. By whom? By God himself; by Jesus who dwells within us; by the Holy Spirit. The Christian life is not a matter of us trying to make ourselves different or better through self-discipline; it is Jesus making us like himself as we abide in him.

Finally, notice that the phrase is written in the plural. *We all* are being transformed—together, as a community of believers in the Lord. We must break out of our self-focused, individualistic way of thinking. Our source of growth is Christ acting in and through all of us, not just in and through each of us by ourselves.

God uses other people to help us grow. Their joy can be the solace to our sorrow. Their words and actions can be the answers to our prayers. Their love and concern can be the healing we need for our pain and heartache. Our brothers and sisters can serve as a very real protection for us on this dangerous pilgrimage.

A friend of mine and his family once took a tour of a zoo. While they were walking through the lion house, the guide warned this father to keep his little daughter close to the group, not to let her stray. "The lions," he said, "always go for the prey that is cut off from the herd."

The Bible issues the same warning: "Your adversary the devil prowls around like a roaring lion, seeking some one to devour" (see 1 Pt 5:8). It is important to our spiritual survival that we "stay close to the group," that we stay in fellowship with the body of Christ.

The stages of intimacy outlined in this chapter are, in a sense, listed in somewhat arbitrary order. The different dynamics I mentioned are very real, and it helps our understanding to review them in a certain order. But in reality, all these stages of growth overlap and interact with each other. They are just different facets of the same jewel, different rooms in the same house.

For example, I first listed "knowing Jesus as Savior," as though it were a sort of elementary first step that we should eventually "grow out of." But in actuality, we never outgrow our need for God's salvation. And we could profitably spend the rest of our lives plumbing the depths of that salvation and what it means for us.

We could say the same thing concerning the concepts of "friendship" and "partnership." These are nothing more than imperfect ways of coming to grips with the great mystery of "Christ in you, the hope of glory" (see Col 1:27). However we break it down, however we try to dissect it and scrutinize it, we are always dealing with something completely beyond our ability to comprehend: the unfathomable commitment God has made to each one of us, to dwell in our hearts, and to change us—day by day, month by month, and year by year, "from one degree of glory to another."

What a friend we have in Jesus! What a friend indeed!

3

Walking with God

NO DOUBT ALL OF US are familiar with the story of Aladdin. A young boy comes across a mysterious brass lamp. Much to his surprise, rubbing the tarnished surface makes a magic genie appear who offers him three wishes. The lad can have anything he wants, just for the asking.

When I was a kid, one of the ways we used to amuse ourselves was to talk about what we would wish for if we had found Aladdin's lamp. Three wishes! Anything we wanted! What would we choose? A million dollars? International celebrity? Astonishing athletic ability? A beautiful mansion? A Rolls Royce? Sooner or later, some wise guy would always come up with the idea that the first thing he'd wish for was ten more wishes!

Other versions of this ancient story suggest that most of us—human nature being what it is—might not choose all that wisely if we were in Aladdin's shoes. One of my children's bedtime story books tells of a poor fisherman who is granted three wishes by a magic fish. (When you think about it, a magic fish is no more bizarre than a genie in a lamp). He quickly resolves not to be too hasty with his wishes. Even while overwhelmed by his good fortune, the man still realizes that careful consideration would produce greater gain.

The fisherman runs home to share the happy news with his wife, who happens to be a bit of a shrew. Smelling their fish stew simmering over the fire, he lapses into imagining the richer fare to be enjoyed in the days ahead. Without thinking, the hungry man mutters, "Ah, I wish we had a big, juicy sausage to go with our supper right now." As soon as the words escape his lips, the succulent sausage appears before their very eyes.

His wife stands appalled at his mental lapse. Doesn't her husband realize how incredibly valuable these wishes are? And there are only three of them! How could he waste one of them on something as trivial as a sausage? Understandably upset, the woman carries on at great length about his stupidity. "Of all the foolish, lame-brained ideas..."

Halfway through this harangue, the fisherman gets so irritated with his wife that he blurts out, "Oh, I wish the sausage were stuck to the end of your nose!" And just like that, the sausage firmly attaches itself to his wife's nose and will not budge no matter how hard they pull. His second wish has been granted.

The fisherman certainly feels sorry for the plight of his pitiful wife, but perhaps she would finally learn a lesson about guarding that tongue of hers. He resumes pondering about how to make the best use of his one remaining wish. As he begins listing the possibilities, his panic-stricken wife interrupts him. "I can't go through life with a sausage stuck to the end of my nose!"

Her plea for mercy brings the poor man to his senses. "I

wish this stupid sausage would just disappear!" And disappear it does. The fisherman and his wife have used up their precious three wishes—with nothing to show for it. They never even got to taste the sausage! But hopefully they learned some helpful lessons to warm the hungry days to come.

MORE THAN A FAIRY TALE

Let's leave the realm of myths and fairy tales and ask the question of you. If you could wish for anything you wanted, what would it be? In fact, if you *knew* God would answer any prayer you prayed, what would you ask of him? A million dollars? A Mercedes Benz? Long life? The ability to heal others? What would *you* ask for?

The fact of the matter is that there is something that God wants to give you more than anything else in the world. It is the reason why he created the human race. It is the reason why he sent the prophets. It is the reason why he ultimately sent his Son, Jesus, to live for us and to die for us. What God wants to give us, more than anything else, is *himself*. He wants to be our friend.

That is the gift God offers each one of us individually. His greatest desire is that we understand this gift, that we receive it from him, and that we enjoy it to the fullest.

To many Christians, friendship with God is an unfamiliar idea. They're used to thinking of God as Creator, as Lord, as Lawgiver, as Judge. These images are true, of course, but they can also tend to be rather cold and unappealing. Even those Christians who do think of God as their Father often picture him as stern and forbidding—the kind of father who can be counted on to fulfill his responsibilities to his family, certainly, but not the kind who would be perceived as kind, as gentle, as warm-hearted—as *a real friend*.

The Bible consistently portrays God as a loving Father who wants his children to enjoy intimacy with him. Again, many of us may find this an unfamiliar or difficult concept. We know that the New Testament portrays Jesus in these terms. But God the Father? The God of the Old Testament? He often seems anything but friendly or close to us.

Yet the Scriptures—right from the start to the very end—portray a God who wants more than anything to offer us genuine friendship with himself. In a sense, the whole Bible is nothing more than the story of God offering this incredible gift to the human race.

Let's look at the beginning, in the book of Genesis. In telling us how God created the universe and the first human beings who inhabited our globe, the opening chapters offer us a number of insights and a foundation for understanding the kind of relationship God wants to have with us.

The expression that Genesis uses to describe God's relationship with Adam and Eve, is that he "walked" with them. That's a way of saying that he desired intimacy or companionship or fellowship with them, and with us as well; he wants us to be by his side as we go about the business of our daily lives.

I see in the opening chapters of Scripture four truths related to walking with God. Please take time to apply these truths to your relationship with God. Is this the way you understand him or approach him? Do you live these truths in your daily life?

First of all, we can walk with God because we are made in his image. Genesis 1:27 says, "So God created man in his own image, in the image of God he created him; male and female he created them." (Incidentally, when Genesis uses the word "man," it means "humankind," the human race, both men and women as made clear at the end of the verse.)

Having been created in the image of God holds several

treasures. For one thing, it means that God has given us the gift of *consciousness*. We can be aware of what he has given us. We are able to see and touch, to taste and smell, to think and feel, and especially to respond to God.

We have also been given the gift of *imagination*, one which allows us to ponder, to reflect, to grasp the implications of God's incredible gift. We have been given the gift of *creativity*. We can actually participate in God's activities. We can take the things God has created—nature, music, color, and all the many facets of the material world—and work with them, responding to God out of love and gratitude.

God has given humankind the gift of *emotion*. We can experience excitement, anger, hope, despair, trust, fear, anticipation, joy, and a myriad of other emotions. Our feelings are certainly not the basis of our relationship with God, but they reinforce and give texture to our relationship with him. They enable us to relate to the world around us in the same way God does. The Bible makes clear that God, too, has emotions.

We also possess a *spiritual dimension*—what is sometimes called a "soul." We are able to perceive and discern the spiritual realm, and to respond to it. Indeed, the deepest hunger of our hearts is for this spiritual food. We worship God in spirit and in truth.

And we have been given the gift of *willpower*, the capacity to choose. This capacity to choose makes us responsible for responding to God's gift of himself. We can accept God's offer of friendship or we can reject it. Our Creator has revealed himself sufficiently so that we can find him if we want, but has also concealed his full glory from those who choose to go their own way in life. Otherwise we would be overwhelmed by the revelation of God. The choice is ours: to find friendship with God or to ignore him and go our own way.

God has made us in his image, after his own likeness. We

share the very nature of God in every way but one: we are finite while God is infinite. We are limited where God is limitless. Nevertheless, we are still able to walk with God—to have intimate fellowship with him—because we are made in his image. We can communicate with him, hear his voice speaking to us, and speak back to him in turn. We can reflect on what God has said and respond accordingly. We can enjoy him. We can choose to walk alongside him and share our lives with him as he shares his life with us.

Second, we are able to walk with God because he has given us "dominion" over his creation. "Then God said, 'Let us make man in our image, after our likeness; and let them have dominion over the fish of the sea, and over the birds of the air, and over the cattle, and over all the earth, and over every creeping thing that creeps upon the earth'" (Gn 1:26).

We fail to fully appreciate the tremendous honor that God bestows by enabling us to participate in his work of ruling over creation. Later in the book of Genesis, we see the first man giving names to all God's creatures: learning to identify them, to respond to them according to their unique natures, to oversee them lovingly and responsibly. What a remarkable opportunity for us to taste God's nature, to experience something of what he himself experiences in his role as sovereign of the universe!

Third, we are able to walk with God because he has called us to bring forth new life. "And God blessed them, and God said to them, 'Be fruitful and multiply, and fill the earth and subdue it'" (Gn 1:28). God's desire was to bring about one huge "garden" filled with men and women who knew him and loved him and walked with him, just as Adam and Eve did. Because he wanted the human race to participate in the process of bringing that desire to reality, God gave us the us the ability to reproduce after our own kind.

New life is brought forth not only physically but also spiritually. We can not only walk with God ourselves, but we can introduce others to a personal relationship with our loving Father. This capacity for spiritual multiplication allows us to participate in the Lord's desire to reconcile people to himself.

God could have by-passed us in this process, but instead he has chosen us to be channels of his grace so that others can find friendship with their Creator. What a privilege! We are not only the objects of his love, but he invites us to be co-workers with him in life. God's relationship with us is not static, but dynamic: it grows, it develops, it has a future, it moves according to God's plan as we bring forth life with and for God.

Fourth, our ability to walk with God is reflected in our ability to walk in friendship with God and others. We see this facet especially illustrated by God creating us male and female. "Then LORD God said, 'It is not good that the man should be alone; I will make him a helper fit for him'" (Gn 2:18). God created both maleness and femaleness to reflect his image in different but complementary ways. Men and women are able to enjoy intimate fellowship despite definite differences. I believe this ability is a sign to us of our capacity as finite creatures to share intimate fellowship with an infinite Creator.

Moreover, the fact that God brought us together to have companionship with one another reflects his own nature as a social being, a God of relationship. We know that God is three persons: Father, Son, and Holy Spirit. Within his divine nature, we see glimpses of the most intimate fellowship possible. In the same way, our human nature carries the possibility of such intimacy in the complementarity of male and female in marriage.

If we are unable to enjoy the God-given capacity for meaningful friendships with others, the same limitations will affect our relationship with God. Perhaps God wants to use this book to highlight the greater *potential* you have for friendship and how you can overcome any barriers that exist in your life to really enjoy your God-given capacity for deep friendships with God and others.

Following the account of creation, God is described as joining Adam and Eve in the garden, walking with them in the cool of the evening (see Gn 3:8). That is what creation was all about: God, man, and woman enjoying intimate companionship with one another. That is *still* what it's all about. For all the wonderful things God has given to us, for all the wonderful things he has created us to be, the incredible bottom line remains that God wants to *walk* with us. He wants us to be his friends.

Of course, what we actually see in this passage from Genesis is how Adam and Even soon make themselves scarce. They "hid from the presence of the LORD God among the trees of the garden." The Lord calls out to them, "Where are you?" (see Gn 3:8-9). I probably don't need to point out to you that when God can't find you, you're not where you ought to be!

OUT OF RANGE

A few years ago, my father needed open-heart surgery. After he was released from the intensive care unit, he was outfitted with a little transmitter that he wore on his belt. The transmitter was connected by wires to a number of contact points on his body, so that the nurses could monitor his vital signs at all times, even when he went for a walk.

About a week after his operation, Dad was feeling a little

frisky and decided to go for a longer-than-usual walk. He boarded the elevator and rode down to the main floor of the hospital. He wandered past the nursery and peeked in at the newborn babies. He checked out the cafeteria. He dropped into the gift shop and browsed through a few magazines.

Suddenly Dad heard a tremendous commotion from the other end of the lobby: people running, carts being pushed out of the way—and someone calling out his name. "McClung! McClung! Where's McClung?" A rather large and red-faced nurse burst around the corner and shouted right in his face, "Are you McClung?"

"Why, yes," my father said. "What's the problem?"

"What's the problem?" the nurse cried. "What's the *problem*? The problem is that you've gotten out of transmitting range of the nurses' station. All your vital signs suddenly disappeared. We thought you were dead!"

That's pretty much what happened with Adam and Eve. They slipped out of range. In his fathomless love and concern, God came looking for them. It's a lesson for us as well. We should always take care not to let our hearts get "out of range" of God. When we do wander off the narrow path, God will always come searching for us. That's how much he loves us. That's how much he wants to walk with us.

In fact, God is willing to go to great lengths to call us back when we wander away. An extraordinary example of this truth occurred not far from where I live in California. A well-known television preacher was out for a drive early one morning along a desert road. Somewhere along the way, he stopped and bought some pornographic magazines, and then picked up a prostitute. Obviously, this man was still in bondage to sin.

When a police car appeared in his rearview mirror, the preacher was overcome with guilt and panicked. As he tried to stuff the incriminating magazines under the seat, the car began to weave across the center line. The policeman thought he was drunk and pulled him over.

It just so happened that a newspaper reporter was monitoring the police radio when the officer called in the incident. Recognizing the famous preacher's name, the news of his escapade soon traveled coast-to-coast, even around the world.

Now here was a gifted minister of the gospel whose outreach was taking in one hundred fifty million dollars a year! Hundreds of thousands of people were being touched by his television show each week. Who knows how many people came to the Lord and were saved as a result of his preaching? And yet the Lord took it all away: the money, the ministry, the fame.

Why? Because he *loves* him. God loves this man so much that he was willing to put him through excruciating embarrassment—and I might add, in the process, to bring shame upon his own name as well—in order to rescue the evangelist from his sins. To God, friendship with a person is far more important than what we do for him or how well we perform.

I wonder how long God had been striving with this man to bring him into pure friendship with himself? But the preacher wouldn't turn from his sins. When he had wandered out of range of God's voice, the Lord's arm was not too short to save. After convicting him and warning him repeatedly, God reached out to him in an unmistakable way: by taking away his ministry.

GOD'S GIFT: GIVEN, RECEIVED, BUT NOT EARNED

The thing we seem to have the hardest time grasping is that God offers his friendship *as a gift*. We don't have to earn it. We don't have to do anything to "deserve" it. In fact, we can never earn it or deserve it no matter how hard we try. God just gives it to us because he loves us.

That, of course, is *not* what the devil would have us believe. No sooner does God offer us the gift of his friendship, no sooner do we accept it, than the devil comes along with his lies. "You don't deserve this. You have to do things to demonstrate that you're worthy of it."

Isn't that what happened to Adam and Eve in the garden? God set before them all the wonders of his creation, all the wonders of his love. Then the devil said, "Well, that's all very nice—but there's more. If you'll just eat the fruit of this tree, you'll *really* become like gods."

Haven't you heard that same voice whispering in your ear? "If you'd just pray more, you'd really be spiritual. If you'd just read the Bible more, you'd really become holy. If you'd just fast more, and give more money, and spend more time out witnessing, God would love you a lot more. If you'd just have longer 'quiet times' every morning...."

Sound familiar? That last line about "quiet time" sounds very familiar to me. One of the first things I was taught as a young Christian was that I should set aside some time every day to be with the Lord. I read books and listened to tapes and heard sermons on the importance of taking a daily quiet time. My goal was to spend one solid hour every day with the Lord, reading Scripture, praying, and listening to his voice. If I put in my hour's worth on a particular day, then I knew I was spiritual. If not...

Do you see what's wrong with this way of thinking? Heaven knows there's nothing wrong with spending quiet time with the Lord every day. But for me, it had gotten all out of perspective. It was something I was doing to try to earn God's favor. If I only spent forty-five minutes with the Lord, I felt I didn't really deserve to walk with him. If I overslept in the morning, I'd eventually have a "quiet-time attack" later in the day: "Oh, no! I missed my quiet time! Now what am I going to do?"

I'm delighted to be able to report to you that I have been delivered from "quiet-time" religion. Not that I don't pray any more—quite the contrary. I *love* to spend time with the Lord. If it can be for an hour in the morning, that's great. If it's for some other period of time, at some other time of day, that's fine too. I love to talk to the Lord, not just during my quiet time, but all day long, wherever I am, whatever I'm doing. I sometimes joke with people that I feel sorry for them if they only have one hour to be with God, instead of twenty-four!

HEART TO HEART

Why are we so susceptible to trying to earn God's friendship? We are deeply aware of how much we have failed God, so we try to overcome our guilt and shame by showing God how sincere we are, how sorry we are. In a word, we feel we have to perform for God, to show him we mean business. So we look for rules to follow, for standards to meet, for goals to achieve. And all the time God is saying, "Let's just walk together. I don't want your accomplishments. I want your heart. My friendship is a gift. You don't deserve it, and you cannot earn it. I want to give it to you because I love you."

I had an experience with my daughter, Misha, several years ago that gave me a glimpse of this truth from God's point of view. When she began middle school, the first school-wide activity was a dance. My daughter came bursting into my study one afternoon and told me about it with great excitement. "Can I go?" Misha asked.

I really felt torn. On the one hand, as a father I was not very open to her going to a dance at twelve years of age! I knew enough about school dances to be legitimately concerned for her well-being. On the other hand—having been teaching and preaching against legalism for years—I knew that going to a school dance isn't inherently sinful. I felt that trying to lay down hard-and-fast rules like "Thou shalt not go to dances" could be counterproductive in the long run.

But on the *other* hand (I think parents are entitled to more than two hands when it comes to sorting out these kinds of issues), I am, after all, a Christian minister. A preacher. The head of a missionary organization. Someone that other people look to for guidance. What kind of message would I send if I let my daughter go to a school dance?

Meanwhile, Misha is gazing at me expectantly. She doesn't want to play therapist and help her father sort out his emotional conflicts. She wants an answer. Probably a part of her wants me to say no. But a larger part of her wants me to say yes.

So how do I answer her?

"Misha," I reply, "I'm not going to say yes *or* no."

She looks up at me with a puzzled expression. With more than a hint of exasperation in her voice, Misha shoots back, "Why not?"

"Because what I want is not just to give you a simple answer and send you on your way. I don't want us to operate on the basis of rules. I want to touch your heart. And I want you to touch *my* heart. Once that's happened, we'll pray and ask the Lord what he thinks about this particular dance, and we'll do whatever he says."

We had a long talk—a very long talk. After a few hours, and more than a few tears, my daughter and I finally had a meeting of our hearts. "I think I understand," Misha said. "You care about me. You love me. You just want to be my friend, and you're genuinely concerned about what could happen to me."

"That's it," I said. "You've got it. I can give you rules and regulations, but that's not what I want the most. I may not always be around when you need me. I want to equip you with values and principles that will help you turn to the Lord and make a good decision for yourself. Are you ready to do that?"

Misha swallowed hard and said she was.

"All right, then," I said. "You understand my concerns, my struggles. You understand that I trust you, but also that I worry about you. You understand my heart, and I think you feel I understand your heart. We've talked together. Now let's pray. Let's ask Jesus."

A while later my daughter came back. "Dad," she said, "I think Jesus said I shouldn't go."

And that's just how it happened. Misha and I went through that process a good many times during her high school days. We took a lot of walks in the "school-dance garden"—not just on this issue, but many others as well. We'd walk and talk together until we had touched each other's hearts, and then turn to the Lord together.

I believe the Lord wants it to be that way between himself and us. So often we want rules from God: "Tell me what I can do and what I can't do. Then I'll be secure. I'll know when I'm okay and when I'm not. I'll know what I have to do to gain your acceptance."

We want answers, but God wants our hearts. He wants to speak to us, to touch us, to hold us close. "I'm with you. I love you. You're not just another item on my agenda, another question to answer, another policy issue to resolve. You're my son, my daughter. I want to walk with you. And I want to teach you my ways, my character. I don't want to give you rules, but I want you to grow into maturity so you can discern for yourself what is right and wrong, wise or unwise."

One time I was teaching on this topic when a young lady

in the crowd stood up in the back of the room and burst into tears. "But if this is true," she said, "I won't know what I'm supposed to *do*. I'll feel so insecure."

I understood this young girl's reaction, but I found it sad. She had been given rules all her Christian life. The thought of walking with God without such guiding rules made her feel deeply insecure. I gently explained that God had something greater for her, he wanted her to walk with *him*.

Our security is in Jesus, not in rules! He wants a relationship with us. He wants to give us the gift of friendship with himself. He wants to walk with us. And when we accept his gift and let him walk with us, when we stop trying to deserve his favor and earn his love, surrounding issues resolve themselves much more readily in the light of his presence.

Let's look more closely at the character of the God who wants to be our friend, and what the Scriptures teach us about how God has sought throughout the ages to find friendship with man.

4

God's Plan for the Ages

T HE ENTIRE BIBLE IS THE STORY OF God's reaching out to humankind with his gift of friendship. We've already looked briefly at Genesis. But what about the rest of the Scriptures? Let's do a quick overview and see how the theme of friendship with God is developed in each section of God's word. We'll look at the Bible in terms of categorizing the various kinds of books it contains: the law, the history books, the prophets, the books of poetry, the Gospels, and Paul's epistles.

GOD IN THE LAW

When we speak of the *law*, we are speaking primarily of the first five books of the Bible: Genesis, Exodus, Leviticus, Numbers, and Deuteronomy. To many people, this particular portion of Scripture seems *least* oriented to the idea of a God who offers friendship to those who rebelled against him. We see God handing down the Ten Commandments. We read lengthy and detailed "rules and regulations" concerning almost every aspect of life.

Why *did* God give the Ten Commandments to his people and establish the law? Was it to place restrictions on our activities? Was it to spell out what we had to do in order to receive God's favor and enjoy his friendship? Was it to mark out a clearly-defined route by which we could work our way toward holiness? Was it (as some people honestly believe, though they might never have the nerve to say it) to provide God with a handy way to decide who goes to heaven and who goes to hell, a kind of divine calculator?

> When your son asks you in time to come, "What is the meaning of the testimonies and the statutes and the ordinances which the LORD our God has commanded you?" then you shall say to your son,... "The LORD commanded us to do all these statutes, to fear the LORD our God, for our good always, that he might preserve us alive, as at this day."
>
> Dt 6:20-24

Notice that one of the words this passage uses to describe the law is *testimonies*. The law serves as testimony to what God is like. God gave the law, not to punish or restrict us, but as an expression of his heart, of his character. He wanted us to be able to know what he was like. Think about it for a minute: what would be worse than knowing that a Supreme Being existed, one who was Master of the universe and Lord of all, one in whom your eternal destiny rested—and not having any idea what he was like or what pleased and displeased him?

When we view the law as an expression of God's character, that he gave the law for our protection and blessing, we begin to glimpse these seemingly dry rules and regulations as an expression of his love, his mercy to humankind. God's intention in giving us the law was to protect us, to *help* us to enjoy a relationship with himself. "Hear, therefore, O Israel, and be careful to do them; that it may go well with you, and that you may multiply greatly, as the LORD, the God of your fathers, has promised you, in a land flowing with milk and honey" (Dt 6:3).

God's motives in giving the law centered around pointing us toward the friendship that he wanted to offer us, keeping us from the things that would come between himself and us, and preserving us from disobedience and the consequences of sin. His deepest motive was to keep us close to himself, so that he might bless us and love us and bestow his good gifts upon us. "In time to come," he would offer us "a still more excellent way." But the law was designed "for our good always." It was designed to lead us into friendship with God himself.

GOD IN THE HISTORY BOOKS

Much of the Old Testament recounts stories of the people of Israel and how God dealt with them through the centuries. This category includes such books as Chronicles, First and Second Samuel, First and Second Kings, Esther, Nehemiah, and others. More than anything, we see a history of God's faithfulness to his people. He makes a covenant with them, one which illustrates his great love no matter how many times they disobey him or bring dishonor upon his name.

Many of the stories are included precisely because they yield a glimpse of what God himself is like. One of my favorites is about a young man named Mephibosheth, the son of Jonathan, who in turn was the son of Saul, Israel's first king.

Mephibosheth led a difficult life. When he was only five years old, word came that his grandfather, King Saul, had been defeated in battle along with his father, Jonathan. A new king—David—had ascended to the throne. In those days, all those in the family of a deposed monarch were routinely put to death so they would not pose a threat to the new dynasty.

When Saul and Jonathan were deposed, Mephibosheth would be considered an heir to the throne. The nursemaid caring for the young boy feared for his life. "He was five years old when the news about Saul and Jonathan came from Jezreel; and his nurse took [Mephibosheth] up, and fled; and, as she fled in her haste, he fell, and became lame" (2 Sm 4:4).

And so Mephibosheth endured life as a crippled fugitive, constantly fearing for his life, hiding from a king who—he could only assume—was bent on destroying him.

But David turned out to be a different sort of king. In fact, David had many years earlier sworn an oath of friendship to Mephibosheth's father, Jonathan. Recognizing that it was the Lord's plan to place David on the throne instead of his own father, Jonathan had pleaded with his friend: "show me the loyal love of the LORD, that I may not die; and do not cut off your loyalty from my house for ever. When the LORD cuts off every one of the enemies of David from the face of the earth, let not the name of Jonathan be cut off from the house of David" (1 Sm 20:14-16). David had wholeheartedly agreed to Jonathan's request.

Many years passed. After the death of Saul and Jonathan, David had become firmly established as king. He had won the hearts of the people. He had expanded the boundaries of the kingdom from six thousand to more than sixty thousand square miles. He had restored the true worship of God to Jerusalem. He had united the people, triumphed over his enemies, and ushered in an era of peace and prosperity.

Overwhelmed by all the Lord's goodness to him and eager to share it, David thinks back to his promise to Jonathan: "And David said, 'Is there still any one left of the house of Saul, that I may show him kindness for Jonathan's sake?'" (2 Sm 9:1).

Imagine! We might expect a monarch to question, "Are there any enemies left for me to destroy?" David instead asks whether anyone remains to whom he can show kindness. One of David's servants provides the answer.

> Ziba said to the king, "There is still a son of Jonathan; he is crippled in his feet." The king said to him, "Where is he?"... Then King David sent and brought him.... And Mephibosheth the son of Jonathan, son of Saul, came to David, and fell on his face and did obeisance.... And David said to him, "Do not fear; for I will show you kindness for the sake of your father Jonathan, and I will restore to you all the land of Saul your father; and you shall eat at my table always." 2 Sm 9:3-8

The Bible calls David "a man after God's own heart." This story provides a touching glimpse into the heart of God. Like David, God is not mean, or vindictive, or stingy with his love. If anything, he is always on the lookout for ways to demonstrate his faithfulness and love. "For if you return to the LORD, your brethren and your children will find compassion.... For the LORD your God is gracious and merciful, and will not turn his face from you, if you return to him" (2 Chr 30:9).

Throughout the history books of the Bible, we stare amazed as the people of Israel turn away from him again and again. Even so, God remained gracious and merciful, and restored them to friendship with himself. And he responds in the same way toward each one of us.

GOD IN THE PROPHETS

The lives and ministries of the prophets show forth God's character and nature in stark contrast to other figures in the Bible. Never passive or bland, the prophets dynamically present the case for a God who deeply cares for his people. One of my favorites is Hosea, who issued this plaintive plea to the Israelites: "Come, let us return to the LORD;/ for he has torn, that he may heal us;/ he has stricken, and he will bind us up./ After two days he will revive us;/ on the third day he will raise us up,/ that we may live before him./ Let us know, let us press on to know the LORD;/ his going forth is sure as the dawn;/ he will come to us as the showers,/ as the spring rains that water the earth" (Hos 6:1-3).

What a magnificent statement of trust in a God who has shown himself to be a faithful friend! Hosea knows that he and his countrymen are going through a time of hardship. Indeed, to some degree they are enduring such suffering at God's hands, as a consequence of their sinfulness.

But Hosea knows that God is not out to destroy his people, nor does he send his servants the prophets with a message of gloom and doom. Hosea knows that though God has torn them, he does this because he wants to heal them; though he has struck them, he wants to bind them up, to revive them, to raise them up.

Jeremiah, too, uttered a message undergirded by a sure sense of God's commitment to covenant relationship with his people. "Thus says the LORD: 'Let not the wise man glory in his wisdom, let not the mighty man glory in his might, let not the rich man glory in his riches; but let him who glories glory in this, that he understands and knows me, that I am the LORD who practice steadfast love, justice, and righteousness in the earth; for in these things I delight, says the LORD'" (Jer 9:23-24).

The mission of the prophets was not, as we often think, primarily to foretell the future—though they certainly did that on occasion. No, their mission was to reveal the heart of God toward his people. And even when the prophetic message included warnings and denunciations of sin, the heart of a loving

God shone through clearly. A tender and merciful God who wanted more than anything to be the faithful friend of his chosen people.

GOD IN THE POETRY BOOKS

The preeminent book of poetry in the Bible is, of course, the Psalms—most of which were written by David. Many are lyric tributes to the love and kindness and mercy of God. David had personally experienced the Lord as a rock of refuge, a shield from the heartaches and calamities of life.

> The LORD is a stronghold for the oppressed,
>   a stronghold in times of trouble....   **Ps 9:9**

Surely only someone who had known God as his faithful friend could have written Psalm 18:

> This God—his way is perfect;
>   the promise of the LORD proves true;
>   he is a shield for all those who take refuge in him.
> For who is God, but the LORD?
>   And who is a rock, except our God?   **Ps 18:30-31**

We are all familiar with Psalm 23, David's celebration of God's tender care for him.

> The LORD is my shepherd, I shall not want;
>   he makes me lie down in green pastures.
> He leads me beside still waters;
>   he restores my soul.
> He leads me in paths of righteousness
>   for his name's sake.

Even though I walk through the valley of the shadow of
    death,
    I fear no evil;
for thou art with me;
    thy rod and thy staff,
    they comfort me.

Thou preparest a table before me
    in the presence of my enemies;
thou anointest my head with oil,
    my cup overflows.
Surely goodness and mercy shall follow me
    all the days of my life;
and I shall dwell in the house of the LORD
    for ever.

Even in the depths of discouragement, David could say:

I waited patiently for the LORD;
    he inclined to me and heard my cry.
He drew me up from the desolate pit,
    out of the miry bog,
and set my feet upon a rock,
    making my steps secure.
He put a new song in my mouth,
    a song of praise to our God.   Ps 40:1-3

David understood that God was not primarily interested in
religious activity, but in the condition of our hearts. After his
terrible sin with Bathsheba, David admitted:

For thou hast no delight in sacrifice;
    were I to give a burnt offering, thou wouldst not be
        pleased.
The sacrifice acceptable to God is a broken spirit;

a broken and contrite heart, O God, thou wilt not
despise.   Ps 51:16-17

In the psalms, David pays poetic homage to the full range of
God's attributes: his justice, his holiness, his might, his power.
But more than anything, David sings of God's mercy, his tenderness, his steadfast love and faithfulness toward his people.
Underlying all of David's songs is his rock-solid certainty that
the God to whom he sings is a God of love, the true and faithful friend of all those who trust in him.

GOD IN THE GOSPELS

Of course, the definitive demonstration of God's driving
determination to befriend us is the gospel—the overwhelming
fact that he became one of us, came to live among us, and died
to take upon himself the punishment for our sinfulness. Jesus
himself was the ultimate expression of God's desire for intimacy with us. Not surprisingly, many of his parables and teach-
ings drive home this point.

An especially enlightening sequence of events is recorded in
the Gospel of Matthew. In the nineteenth chapter we read of
Jesus' encounter with a person we have come to know as "the
rich young ruler." Intensely concerned about his spiritual condition, this man has come to Jesus with an urgent question.
"Teacher," he says, "what good deed must I do to have eternal
life?"

Perhaps you can perceive in the very terms of his question
that this young man is on the wrong track. He asks, "What
good deed must I do?" When he and Jesus begin to discuss the
commandments of God, the young man rattles off his religious résumé. He claims to have kept the commandments,
every last one of them, ever since he was a child. "All these I

have observed; what do I still lack?"

"If you would be perfect," Jesus replies, "go, sell what you possess and give to the poor, and you will have treasure in heaven; and come, follow me" (Mt 19:21).

Doesn't this reply strike you as rather harsh? Here is this utterly sincere young man who wants to know how to please God. He has clearly worked hard to keep all the commandments. But he is unwilling to rest on his laurels. Now he is asking what *more* he can do! The rich young ruler reminds me of a straight-A student asking the teacher for extra-credit assignments. And what does Jesus tell him? Sell everything you have! Give it all away!

Jesus issues a hard word, and the young man receives it as such: "When the young man heard this he went away sorrowful; for he had great possessions." Jesus observes to his disciples that "it is easier for a camel to go through the eye of a needle than for a rich man to enter the kingdom of heaven."

What a shocking statement! "When the disciples heard this," Matthew writes,"they were greatly astonished, saying, 'Who then can be saved?'" Can't you just hear the incredulity in their voices?

But in fact, they have just begun to touch on the point of the whole incident. Jesus simply replies, "With men this is impossible, but with God all things are possible."

Do you see? "With men this is impossible." There is nothing the rich young ruler could do—and nothing you or I could ever do—to earn God's favor or to deserve his friendship. That was precisely the young man's mistake—as it is so often our mistake. His entire approach to knowing God was to do things for God. Jesus was trying to expose this faulty basis of his relationship with God. There was *nothing* he could do to earn friendship or relationship with God: it is God's gift!

Jesus was deliberately responding to the rich young ruler in his own terms, pressing his own thinking to the limit, trying to show him that eternal life and friendship with God were not within his power to earn. *Of course* it was beyond him to sell all his possessions—that was the whole point! And even if he did sell everything, Jesus wanted him to come face to face with the impossibility of pleasing God through religious efforts, doing good deeds for God as a basis for relationship with God.

Unfortunately, the rich young ruler seems to have missed the point. So, at first, did the disciples. Peter immediately jumps in and says, "Lo, we have left everything and followed you. What then shall we have?" This outspoken disciple is arguing, in effect, "Well, maybe that guy wasn't man enough to do what was necessary, but we sure are!"

Jesus replies: "Every one who has left houses or brothers or father or mother or children or lands, for my name's sake, will receive a hundredfold, and inherit eternal life" (Mt 19:29).

The Lord is not enunciating a precise formula, like some sort of spiritual investment ratio guaranteed to increase your eternal portfolio. He is saying that God's reward is out of all proportion to what Peter or any of the disciples could ever do for him, to any sacrifice they could ever make. He is telling us that God's reward system is not based on our merit, but on his grace. Friendship is not based on our performance, but on God's goodness.

And then, as was his custom, Jesus drives home the point by telling a parable. Let's look at it in some depth.

For the kingdom of heaven is like a householder who went out early in the morning to hire laborers for his vineyard. After agreeing with laborers for a denarius a day, sent them into his vineyard. And going out about the third hour he saw others standing idle in the market place; and to them he said, "You go into the vineyard too, and whatever is right I will give you." So they went. Going out again about the sixth hour and the ninth hour, he did the same. And about the eleventh hour he went out and found others standing;

and he said to them, "Why do you stand here idle all day?" They said to him, "Because no one has hired us." He said to them, "You go into the vineyard, too." And when evening came, the owner of the vineyard said to his steward, "Call the laborers and pay them their wages, beginning with the last, up to the first." And when those hired about the eleventh hour came, each of them received a denarius. Now when the first came, they thought they would receive more; but each of them also received a denarius. And on receiving it they grumbled at the householder, saying, "These last worked only one hour, and you have made them equal to us who have borne the burden of the day and the scorching heat." But he replied to one of them, "Friend, I am doing you no wrong; did you not agree with me for a denarius? Take what belongs to you, and go; I choose to give to this last as I give to you. Am I not allowed to do what I choose with what belongs to me? Or do you begrudge my generosity?" So the last will be first, and the first last.   Mt 20:1-16

The obvious point of the story is that the householder rewarded his workers not on the basis of what they had earned, but simply on the basis of what he had determined he wanted to give them. Perhaps he arrived at the sum because that particular amount of money would allow the workers to feed their families for a day. Perhaps those who worked all day really *were* underpaid, as they seem to imply. But perhaps the workers were all *over*paid, receiving far more than they could possibly have earned on the basis of an hourly wage.

That, at least, is the case with us. We have all received far, far more than we could ever hope to earn by our own efforts.

The attitude of the complaining workers is intriguing. Many of us, perhaps, cannot relate to the illustration of day laborers. Jerry Bridges, in his book, *Transforming Grace*, sheds more light on the issue by using a more contemporary example:

At a certain state university there was a freshman English class with the typical variety of students. On the one hand there were a few conscientious and well-disciplined students who had learned good study habits in high school, who consistently did assignments, studied well for tests, and turned in well-prepared term papers on time.

At the opposite end of the spectrum were the typical party boys who did just enough work to get by. They rarely did assignments, hardly studied for tests, and never turned in a term paper on time. And, as is typical in such a class, the vast majority of students were somewhere in between.

At last final exam day arrived. As expected, the disciplined students all did well and party boys all did poorly. After a couple days, the professor posted the grades outside his office door. As the students crowded around to see what grade they had received, they were all stunned to see that everyone in the class had received an "A." The party boys could hardly believe their good fortune, and the good students were outraged to realize that those who deserved to fail had received the same top grade as they had.[1]

Seems unfair, doesn't it? Well, now we know how those laborers felt who had worked in the hot sun all day long. If our orientation is to think purely in terms of earning our reward, the generous grace of God can be quite scandalous.

Jesus knew what he was doing when he told the parable of the householder. I have known diligent, lifelong Christians who became resentful toward new converts who seemed to be getting especially blessed by the Lord. Their attitude was precisely the same as the workmen who complained to the householder: "It's not fair, Lord! How can you bless them so abundantly? Why, they just came into the kingdom last week!"

But "fairness" really has nothing to do with it. Indeed, we should fervently hope that God never decides to be "fair" with us. Believe me, the one thing none of us wants is for God to give us what we truly deserve!

There is a grand extravagance to God's love for us. Not only does he not give us what we truly deserve, but he offers to us what we don't deserve, what we could never have dared to ask for, what we could never have even imagined possible: intimate friendship with himself.

GOD IN THE LETTERS OF PAUL

Perhaps no writer in the entire Bible understands more clearly the gift of God's friendship than the great apostle. Raised in the "confidence in the flesh" (Phil 3:4), Paul was a Jew above other Jews, a persecutor of Christians, a zealous practioner of the law.

But God broke into Paul's life and saved him from religion and slavery to the law. Paul was led into the Arabian desert for three years, probably to cleanse his mind of his total dependence on Judaism. God wanted to show him that God was not the God of the religious ("the Jews only"—Rom 3:29), but of all mankind. He revealed to Paul that he longed for friendship with those he created in his image, and that though humankind had rejected, ridiculed, and ignored him, he was determined to bring all those who will into friendship with himself.

Overwhelmed with this revelation, Paul could not keep silent (Gal 1:11-16).

Therefore, since we are justified by faith, we have peace with God through our Lord Jesus Christ. Through him we have obtained access to this grace in which we stand, and we rejoice in our hope of sharing the glory of God... because God's love has been poured into our hearts through the Holy Spirit, which has been given to us.   **Rom 5:1, 2, 5b**

Paul knows that we were made for relationship with God. God has made us for friendship. The history of salvation—indeed, the history of humankind as told from Genesis through Revelation—resounds with this triumphant theme. God has created us in his own image so that we might know him and reign with him. He has created us with a capacity for relationship that finds its genuine expression only in a loving relationship with him.

Standing in the center of all God has done is his Son Jesus. All history focuses upon Christ, the one who makes friendship with God an attainable reality for us. As we shall see in the following chapters, it is Jesus who redeems us from our fallen state and restores us to fellowship with God. It is Jesus who rescues us from our warped and distorted old identities, and who enables us to receive a new identity from God, indeed, a whole new relationship with God.

5

Religion: A Case of Mistaken Identity

A S ALWAYS, the alarm went off much earlier than he was
ready for. He swung his arm in a full arc toward the
bedside table, groping until he found the little button on top
of the clock and put an end to the maddening buzz. Then
slumping back down into the covers with his eyes closed, he
tried to put the pieces together in his mind.

He had been on the road for—it seemed like forever. Days.
Weeks. An endless procession of cookie-cutter motel rooms.
The same saggy mattresses, the same swivel-base televisions,
the same nondescript floral wallhangings. The same jarring
alarm clocks that always went off too early.

What time was it? He had no idea. Where was he? He
couldn't remember. At the moment, he wasn't sure *who* he
was, let alone where.

The only thing he *did* feel some certainty about was that he
was hungry. Well, that was at least a logical starting point: get
something to eat. His hand groped across the little bedside

table again until he found the phone. He wedged the receiver in between his head and the pillows, and punched the "0" button. Three rings... four... five... finally an answer.

"Operator."

"Uhh, yeah... listen, connect me with room service, would you?"

"I beg your pardon, sir?"

"Room service. I want to order breakfast."

There was a pause. "I'm sorry, sir. I'm not able to help you with that. You'll have to dial Information."

He groaned. *Why me?* he thought. "Listen, operator, I just want to order some breakfast. Is it too early to do that?"

"Well, no sir, I'm sure it's not, but..."

But what? he thought. *What's her problem?* "Look, I'm very tired and I'm very hungry, and—"

"Yes, sir. I can understand that you're tired. But I think that if you'll turn on the light and look around, you'll discover that you're not in a motel."

He bolted upright in bed, switched on the light, and looked around him. She was right. He was at home, in his own bedroom.

This true story actually happened to a friend of mine at the end of a long trip. He was so exhausted that for a moment he really did forget who he was and where he was. He had reached a *real* operator, not just a motel operator. It was a case of mistaken identity.

My friend's confusion was funny. But many Christians suffer from a much more serious case of mistaken identity. When we accept Christ, we don't fully grasp who we are as children of God, as *friends* of God. As a result, we expend much of our energy striving, performing, implementing spiritual formulas, doing spiritual gymnastics, trying to attain something that has already been given to us, trying to earn something that is already ours. Religion is a substitute for relationship and it causes us to try to *become* something *we already are.*

We mistakenly draw our identity from whether or not we have achieved what we have told ourselves we need to achieve, rather than from the gift God has given us. Even when we hear the good news that God offers us genuine friendship with himself as a free gift, we have a hard time believing it. "Not *me*," we think. "Somebody else, maybe. But not me." Sadly, we become another case of mistaken identity.

NICKELS FROM HEAVEN

I once read about an interesting experiment conducted by a college psychology class. After handing each of his students a roll of nickels, the professor sent them out to local shopping malls and street corners with instructions to simply give each of the coins away to the people who walked by. The students weren't allowed to explain what was going on, nor to answer any questions. They were just supposed to give away the nickels, no strings attached.

Sounds great, doesn't it? Free money! Where do I sign up?

But a funny thing happened. *People refused to take the money.* Can you believe it? They wouldn't accept a free nickel! Some of them asked questions: "Who are you? Why are you doing this? What's it all about? What's the catch?" But most of them just sheepishly ducked their heads and slid past in silence.

What if the amount had been, say, a thousand dollars, or even a cool million? Can you picture it? You're walking down the street—minding your own business, of course—when someone walks up to you and says, "This suitcase has a million dollars in it. I'd like you to have it. Here."

How would you react? I suspect most of us would be just like the people in the experiment. We'd immediately be suspicious. "Who is this guy?" we'd wonder. "Why's he doing this?

Is this drug money? Why is he trying to give money to *me*? What's the catch?"

The tragedy is that so many of us react this way to God's free gift of himself. We can't believe it's for real. We can't bring ourselves to simply accept it. "Surely there must be a catch," we think. "Surely there must be *something* that I have to do to earn this."

We have such a strong performance orientation that we find it difficult to accept a gift for what it is—even when it comes from God. "Okay, God," we say. "What do I have to do in return for this? Pray more? Have better quiet times? Teach a Sunday school class? Hand out tracts? Give more money?"

Or we think, "There must be some mistake. He must have the wrong person. This must be intended for somebody else."

Admit it: haven't you often felt that way?

I happen to enjoy receiving humorous greeting cards. The crazier the better. My family knows this, so every time Father's Day or my birthday rolls around, they try to outdo each other in coming up with outlandish cards. I remember one that I received from my daughter, Misha. On the front, in bold type, it said,

> I believe that some people were born for a noble purpose. I believe that the destinies of a few special human beings are of a higher order, that fate intervenes in the lives of an elite group of unique individuals and catapults them onto a loftier plane of existence.

I was so impressed with this high-sounding sentiment, my chest started to swell a bit with pride. Then I opened the card and read the message on the inside: *"I believe you are not one of these people. Happy Birthday."*

I loved this card! But the tragedy is that so many of us, deep down inside, really do think about ourselves that way when it comes to God. We really do believe that there are people who enjoy a privileged status in God's eyes. People who are his special friends, his favorites. People he has blessed in a special way, people he has drawn into a unique relationship with himself. *But we also believe that we are not one of these people.*

But we are! That is the message of this book. Indeed, as we saw in the last chapter, it is the message of the whole Bible. *You and I* are people whom God has offered a special, intimate relationship with himself. The fact that we do not realize it— that we actually *resist* receiving his gift and acknowledging that as redeemed Christians we are his friends—is a tragic case of mistaken identity.

Most of us realize God wants to be our friend. But we can also recognize that this deeper level of life in Christ, of friendship with God, is something we are missing. Could there be a fullness, a warmth, a depth, a joy that is ours by grace and yet somehow be missing out on this blessing?

Has this question haunted you year after year? The pathways of self-effort and self-condemnation become well-worn. We may try the "confess-it and possess-it" approach, or the seven-step plan, or the five-fold truth to spiritual maturity. We listen to tapes and attend conferences; we subscribe to Christian magazines and tune into charismatic speakers. But we gradually grow weary of all the effort, the organizations, the methods.

Deep in our being we know we are created for God, for deeper relationship with our Creator. We believe what the Scriptures teach us about a relationship so revolutionary, so startling, yet freely available to us. We even taste it from time to time in those special but ever so rare moments of closeness with God. Yet, somehow, on a daily level, we are missing what is ours. Is it because we have a mistaken idea about who we are, who we were created to be?

QUACK, QUACK—I'M A CHICKEN!

Once upon a time (yes, this is going to be a sort of fairy tale, or more of a parable, really), there was a farmer who, among other things, raised chickens. One day as he was out on his tractor he passed by a small pond. Next to the water he found the scattered remains of a female duck—apparently killed by a fox.

The farmer also came upon a nest of duck eggs that the fox had somehow missed. He carefully scooped up the eggs, carried them back to the barn, and placed them in the nest of the barnyard hen. The trick worked. The old mother cluck somehow got the idea that the eggs were hers. As maternal instinct kicked in, she sat on the eggs, just as she always did, until they finally hatched.

The ducklings never knew the difference. They assumed that the old hen was their mother and followed her around the barnyard just the way baby chicks would usually do. The rest of the chickens didn't know the difference either. They readily accepted the baby ducklings as members of the family.

Until one day, when a summer rainstorm had left a huge puddle of water in the barnyard. The chickens carefully picked their way around the edges of the water. But without even thinking about it, the ducklings just waddled over and started paddling around.

The mother hen was greatly alarmed. "Get out of there this instant!" she frantically cried. "You can't do that. You're chickens. You'll drown!" Reluctantly the ducklings left the puddle. The water had felt so good in the hot sun.

But the puddle incident was only the beginning of the ducklings' confusion. They did their best to blend into the surrounding chicken culture, but they continued to suffer embarrassing lapses. Sometimes when they tried to cluck, they quacked instead.

Sometimes when they got excited, they would flap their wings and start to fly—until they remembered that they were chickens, and chickens didn't do that. Their embarrassment slowly grew into frustration and finally deepened into depression. Something wasn't right, and they couldn't figure out what it was.

One night a wise old owl sitting in a nearby tree saw the ducklings and said, "Whoooooooooo... are you?"

"Chickens," they replied sheepishly. (Sorry, I couldn't resist that one.) They were ashamed to admit it. They knew they were not very good representatives of the chicken community.

"Don't be ridiculous," the owl replied. "You're not chickens. You're ducks!"

"What do you mean?" the ducklings replied.

"I mean just what I said," the owl smiled. "You're not chickens. You're not made to cluck and scratch the ground. Haven't you ever felt like swimming across a pond? Haven't you ever felt like spreading your wings and flying away?"

"Yes!" they replied. "Yes, we've felt that way many times. But we were always told that we couldn't. We were always told that we weren't supposed to."

"Horsefeathers!" cried the owl. "You're ducks! You were *made* to swim! You were made to fly!"

The ducklings stared up at the owl in disbelief, then looked around excitedly among themselves.

"Well," the owl finally said, "what are you waiting for?"

This "children's" story makes a point that a lot of grownups need to hear. We are a lot like those ducklings. We are born into a world that considers human beings as nothing more than intelligent animals, referred to by one author as "naked apes." Scientists assure us that we are locked into a material cosmos bound by time and space and the earthly laws of nature.

Already securely tethered to the ground, we are then "reborn" into a Christian world that tells us we cannot "fly."

"You'll calm down after you've been a Christian a few years," we are counseled by countless veterans of spiritual combat. "You'll get over all the excitement and realize we have to face a host of problems and accept a multitude of things we can't do."

But something inside us knows better. Something inside us knows we *were* made for better things. Something inside us senses the existence of a reality that is higher, deeper, more *real* than that which surrounds us in our daily lives.

Something inside us longs to rise above the things of earth and the limitations of mere humanity, to rise above the power of sin and selfishness, to reach out and touch the face of God —to take wings and *fly*, to walk with God, and to abide in his presence and in his love.

Thank God for those few who told us what we have always sensed deep inside: that we *were* made for greater things... indeed fashioned for fellowship with the Creator of the universe. We are not just human animals, organisms evolved from the slime of the earth, but spiritual beings, created in the image and likeness of God, designed to know him and to touch him and to be intimate with him.

Nor are we second class spiritual citizens. We are not "failures" though we may fail; nor are we just "sinners" though we certainly do sin. Nor are we the sum total of our weaknesses and low "self-images;" we are friends of the true and living God! And when that realization bursts upon us, when that awareness takes hold of our hearts, there is only one question left: *What are we waiting for?*

BECOMING SOMEBODY

Actually, the owl in the above story poses a question more profound than it may seem at first. *Who are you?* How would *you* answer that question? How do you really answer that question? How do you see yourself?

Most of us immediately respond in terms of our occupation, in terms of what we *do*. "I'm a housewife," we may say, or a carpenter, or a lawyer, or whatever we happen to be doing at the present time.

Suppose our questioner presses us a bit further. "I'm not asking what you do for a living. I'm asking who you *are*. What is your fundamental identity?"

Now what do you say? "I'm an American... I'm English... well, actually, I guess, I'm Irish, but I was born and raised here, but..."

"No," the questioner again interjects, "I'm not asking you *where* you're from. I'm asking, *who* are you?"

Do you see the problem? We live in a performance-oriented culture where our worth is reckoned—and our very identity determined—by what we do or where we come from. For most of us, if you take away our "doing" identity, we don't really *know* who we are. That's the only way we've ever learned to answer the question.

Almost everything, for as long as we can remember, has boiled down to achievement, to accomplishment, to performance. That is how we move ahead. That is how we "become somebody" in this world—and unfortunately, often even in our own families. *"Behave nicely and we'll be proud of you." "Play harder and maybe you can be in the big leagues some day." "Study harder and maybe you can go to college or university." "Work harder and maybe you can become rich and famous."*

Is it any wonder we take the same approach to our relationship with God? Pray longer, read more Scripture, evangelize more, serve on more committees... and maybe, just maybe, God will be pleased with us.

What a tragedy it is to live our lives suffering from a case of mistaken identity! I once ministered to a young lady who was trying to leave behind a lifestyle of homosexuality. She had heard the gospel and responded to it, had given her life to

Jesus, and experienced a wonderful spiritual rebirth.

But in *her* own eyes, her most basic identity was still, "I am a lesbian." I had to tell her over and over again, "No, that's wrong. That's not *who* you are. It's what you used to *do*, but it's not who you *are*. God doesn't look upon you in terms of your past behavior. He looks upon you in terms of having created you to be his friend, and on the basis of what he has done for you. He looks at you as his daughter. He looks at you as his friend."

It was a struggle, but in time the eyes of that young lady's heart were opened and she began to see the truth of what I told her. She began to understand the tremendous gift that God had given her, the gift of friendship with himself. She began to view herself not as "a lesbian," but as "a child of God."

I perceive a tragic flaw in the teaching and thinking of many Christian books and theologians, an error that seems to pervade evangelical Christianity. A Christian is not merely a person who has received something wonderful from God—whether it is forgiveness, a new life, the gift of heaven, the Holy Spirit, or whatever. The process of conversion is always much more fundamental. "A Christian is a person who has become someone he was not before."[1]

The young lady who sinned by sexual involvement with another woman did not just receive forgiveness when she came to Christ. She became a brand new person. She became someone she was not before, a child of God. As her birthright, she received a whole new identity.

FALSE SELF-IMAGES

What are some of the more common "mistaken identities" that we human beings apply to ourselves? Many of us, like the young lady I just described, define ourselves in terms of our *sin*. In fact, I believe that one of the most significant mistaken identities among Christians is the one that says, "I am a worthless sinner."

Much of Christianity embraces what I call "worm theology." There's even an old hymn that says, "O, what a worm am I." Our Western approach to Christianity is so human-centered that our beginning point is not God and what he has done for us, but ourselves and what we have or have not done for God.

Of course it is true that "all have sinned and fall short of the glory of God" (Rom 3:23). In that sense, we are indeed all sinners. But if we let that reality become our most basic touchstone for who we are, we will inevitably suffer from a severe case of mistaken identity.

We are not just miserable sinners who need to grovel before God and search desperately for some way to win back his favor. We were created by a loving God, created to be especially beloved children who can come to our Father. When we sin or fail him, we can readily receive his forgiveness and mercy.

Some of us define ourselves as *failures*. We focus on some particular area of weakness or limitation, on some instance where we have fallen short of some ideal. We soon turn that into our identity. "I'm fat." "I never finished school." "I'm not married."

Again, some of us may very well be overweight. But that does not equate with who we *are*. Taking our identity from an area of weakness or failure leads us to think of ourselves as someone who can never succeed—who might as well not even try—rather than as someone chosen and beloved by God, who gives us the grace to be everything he calls us to be.

Others see themselves as *unspiritual*. When they hear visiting missionaries telling tales of great exploits for God, they think, "I could never be like them." When they hear people in their church talk about how they pray and read their Bibles two hours every day, they think, "I'm lucky if I can pray two hours a month!"

But the goal of spirituality isn't topping someone else's achievements. The point is living out our friendship with God in ways that are uniquely appropriate to us, being honest about who we are, and growing spiritually one day at a time. God has a spiritual timetable for each and every individual. We will never discover his agenda for our own lives by comparing ourselves to others, but by looking to Jesus. As we respond to his plans for our future—rather than being molded by the expectations of others—we will grow in friendship with God.

Closely related to the "unspiritual" folk are those who see themselves as *immature*. "I can't do anything for God," they say. "I'm just a baby Christian. I still have so much to learn, so much growth to accomplish."

I've known people who have been in the Lord for twenty years who still think of themselves as "baby Christians"! I have known other people who have moved into a fruitful and rewarding relationship with God almost before they've finished drawing their first breath of new life in Christ. The way we perceive ourselves seriously affects our ability to enjoy the intimacy God offers all of us.

Still others draw their identity from their *physical appearance*—usually from aspects of their appearance that they consider inadequate or flawed. They are too fat or too skinny, too tall or too short, too ugly or too beautiful. They have fallen victim to the lie that our society so relentlessly peddles: that appearance is everything. They become unable to see themselves as God sees them.

In the end, I suppose there are as many false self-images as there are people. Each of us, it seems, falls prey to some particular mistaken identity, some distorted perspective of ourselves that robs us of the joy and freedom and peace that come from simply resting in our true identity: as beloved sons and daughters of God.

Struggling with a false sense of who we are is a terrible way to live. We burn endless energy striving to change ourselves, to improve ourselves, to make ourselves into something we're not, or to better ourselves in order to be loved by God.

But a Christian is not just a forgiven sinner who then goes on to develop a "healthy self-image"—the same way the rest of the world does through exercise classes or new clothes or financial success or civic achievements or whatever. Such pursuits may be fine, each in their proper context, but they have nothing to do with *who we are*. The very nature of the gospel is that God gives us a gift. We do not have to improve ourselves or "do something special" in order to obtain it. We simply need to receive it as a wonderful gift from a Father who loves us.

BUT...

I already know what some of you are thinking. "But I *am* a sinner," you say. "It's not just a figment of my imagination, either—I *know* I am. And I know that God isn't exactly pleased by my sin. I know that I've failed God in some important areas of my life. How does that fit in with everything else you've said about God wanting to be my friend?"

Good question. And there's a good answer for it. God isn't ignorant of our sins and weaknesses and failings. And he doesn't ignore them, either, or sweep them under some cosmic rug.

When we began our examination of friendship with God, we looked at how that special relationship was expressed in Scripture. We saw how the book of Genesis makes clear that

God designed us for intimacy with himself from the very beginning. But these first chapters of the Bible also make something else very clear: the human race soon chose to reject God's offer of friendship.

You know the story. God commanded Adam and Eve not to eat of a certain tree in the middle of the garden. But, deceived by Satan, Adam and Eve disobeyed God. They made a tremendously foolish and selfish choice—a choice, by the way, that every single human being since has ratified in his or her own choices and behavior (see Rom 5:12).

Friendship cannot exist without mutual commitment. By opting out of their relationship with God, Adam and Eve in effect dethroned God from his rightful place of supremacy in their lives, and in so doing turned away from the gift of friendship God had offered them.

And so, with great grief and disappointment, God allowed the human race to travel the path they had chosen: the path of sin. The Bible says, "your sins have hid his face from you/ so that he does not hear" (Is 59:2). Men and women died to fellowship with God and became subject to the consequences of their sin: physical decay, sickness, pain, death.

The Scriptures teach that we are separated from God. Each of us has followed that same path chosen by Adam and Eve. "All we like sheep have gone astray;"/ the Bible says, "we have turned each one to his own way;..." (Is 53:6).

For Adam and Eve, intimacy with God became a haunting memory, something in their past that they could remember only vaguely, as through a veil, dimly. For us, intimacy with God is an unrealized, inner yearning. We can't quite put a finger on it, but it's there, like some deep ache or yawning chasm. "As a hart longs/ for flowing streams,/ so longs my soul/ for thee, O God" (Ps 42:1).

In this broken relationship, humankind was the greatest loser, but God has continued to be the greatest sufferer. We are dimly conscious of our need, but we don't fully realize what we're missing. The all-knowing and all-loving Lord possesses full knowledge of the blessings that he intended us to have.

God experiences untold grief as those blessings remain unclaimed by all the individual men and women who are separated from him. "The LORD saw that the wickedness of man was great in the earth, and that every imagination of the thoughts of his heart was only evil continually. And the LORD was sorry... it grieved him to his heart" (Gn 6:5-6).

Now you might think that since humankind was the cause of this ruptured relationship, it would be up to us to take the initiative to make things right, to come to God and apologize. But that's not what has happened. It was God who took the initiative, God who has been the gracious one. "For thou, O Lord, art good and forgiving,/ abounding in steadfast love to all who call on thee" (Ps 86:5).

So often we fail to appreciate the complexity and the delicacy of the task that confronted God as he set about restoring relationship with us. Think for a moment about his predicament. God had offered friendship to humankind, but we said no. He now faced the task of trying to bring the human race to a place where it would be willing, even desirous, of coming back into relationship. But God was not willing to manipulate humanity into doing so.

And there was also the dilemma of human sin. Adam and Eve didn't just politely decline God's offer. Their actions in the garden were not just a "No, thanks," but a haughty rejection of God's gift, a willful violation of what they knew very well to be God's commandment.

Sometimes when their children disobey them, human parents deal with the situation by simply overlooking their behavior, by pretending it never happened. They think, "Well, it was a little thing, really. They didn't really mean it. I can let it pass this time."

Can you see why that option was not open to God? What

Adam and Eve did *wasn't* a little thing, plus it was clear that they really *did* mean it. To make matters even worse, what they did happened on a cosmic stage: all creation knew what they did, and all creation would be witness to how God handled their disobedience.

It would be disastrous for him to ignore it, to say that breaking his commandments was "no big deal." God would be acting in violation of his own nature, because his laws are never just arbitrary "rules and regs" that he jots down in spare moments, but deep expressions of his fundamental character.

Moreover, God would be demonstrating that his own laws carried no weight. To say one thing and then do another would undermine his reliability. Ultimately, such disregard would undermine the very thing God was aiming for: humanity's *desire* to come back into fellowship with himself. Who could desire intimacy with a God whose word could not be trusted?

So God found himself in a delicate situation. His law called for punishing the human race by consigning it to eternal separation. Yet his desire was precisely the opposite: to restore intimate fellowship. What could God do? I heard one man answer that question this way: "Some public event of profound influence must be substituted, one that will be at least as effective in preventing and restraining sin as the punishment of all sinners would have been."

Even as it portrays his mercy, this public event must simultaneously demonstrate that God has not abandoned his justice. Otherwise such an action would devalue divine forgiveness. It must also elicit a certain kind of response from those who have sinned: a frank recognition that they have offended God and rejected his offer of friendship, along with a desire to see the relationship made whole. God's response cannot be merely coercive; it must be something that evokes humility and a heartfelt desire to change.

So what did God do? How did he deal with our sin and at the same time provide for our return to intimacy with him?

THE KING'S DILEMMA

I used to live in Amsterdam. Sightseers to the Netherlands often visit the Queen's Palace, which is located on the main square of Amsterdam. Inside the palace is an extraordinary piece of art: a *bas-relief* mural, almost fifteen feet long, that tells the story of an ancient Greek king named Zaleucas.

Zaleucas had a problem in his kingdom: thievery. He did everything he could think of to put a stop to it. He increased the size and number of his military patrols, but the thievery continued. The king offered rewards to people who turned thieves in to the authorities. Even this had no noticeable effect. Finally, he issued a decree that anyone caught stealing would have both his eyes put out.

The stern decree seemed to work, at least for a while. Fear of the terrible punishment provided a powerful deterrent, and for several weeks there were no reports of thievery anywhere in the kingdom.

Then, inevitably, it happened. One day a messenger came to King Zaleucas with a sad expression on his face. A thief had been caught, he said—caught in the very act of stealing. There was no doubt whatsoever about his guilt. What was worse, it had happened right there in the palace!

King Zaleucas was enraged. How could anyone be so brazen as to break his command, and risk the fierce punishment he had decreed, right in his own palace? He ordered the thief brought to him at once.

The buzz of excitement that filled the king's throne room suddenly shrank to stunned silence when the guilty man was brought forward. The king's face turned ashen as he looked down at the man standing before him. It was his own son, the crown prince! There was no conceivable reason for his behavior, but there was no doubt about it: he was guilty.

The king faced a terrible dilemma. Word had quickly passed through the whole kingdom about what had happened. Everyone knew who the guilty party was, and everyone knew the punishment the king had decreed. What would the king do? Would he keep his word and put out the eyes of his own son? Or would he let him go free—and demonstrate to the entire kingdom that he did not mean what he said, that his laws and decrees were without meaning? What *could* he do? The distraught father ordered his son to be cast into prison while he pondered the matter.

After three days, King Zaleucas summoned his son back to the throne room. He told him he loved him dearly, and could not bear the thought of both his eyes being put out. But at the same time, he had issued an official decree. The king needed to be faithful to his word, to uphold his own standard of justice.

"Therefore," the king solemnly declared, "I have arrived at the following decision. The demands of the law will be satisfied. I will put out one of your eyes—and I will put out one of my own eyes as well."

And the king did exactly what he said. His astonishing action made it abundantly clear to all his subjects that King Zaleucas was a man of integrity. But it also made it clear that he was a man of compassion and mercy. The whole kingdom marvelled at Zaleucas' willingness to sacrifice himself for the love of his son, and for the love of his kingdom.

This story vividly illustrates what God did for humankind. Man and woman had sinned, had disobeyed God: there was no doubt about their guilt. Nor was there any doubt about the punishment God had decreed. But God found a way to uphold his law and yet show mercy to us. He provided a substitute to bear our punishment for us: his Son, Jesus, who on the cross took upon himself the sins of the whole world.

It was God who took the initiative, so that he might reconcile humankind to himself, might bring us back into intimate friendship. It was his way of saying, "Yes, you have sinned. Yes, you have offended me. Yes, you are weak and unspiritual and immature. But I will forgive you. I myself will come and bear the punishment that is rightfully yours. And from now on, when I look at you I will see not the sin and the weakness, but I will see the face of my Son. I will relate to you with precisely the same love and affection and generosity that I hold for him."

That is why all our mistaken identities are just that: mistaken. Even though we are weak and sinful, nevertheless in God's eyes we are accepted. By his own action, he has made it possible for us to be reconciled to him. It is not something we could ever earn. Restoration to fellowship is his gift. It remains only for us to humble ourselves and receive such mind-boggling generosity. When we do, we take on the fullness of our true identity: friends of God.

In the next chapter, we'll look more closely at what this true identity means for us.

6

True Identity:
Who Are We, Really?

I'M NO DIFFERENT FROM ANY OTHER PARENT: I worry about my kids. I long to see them healthy, and happy, and fruitful in life. In particular, I long to see them solidly growing in relationship with God, knowing his love for them, loving him in return, excited about being his children.

So I had to smile the day my daughter, Misha—who was twelve years old at the time—returned from youth camp so enthusiastic that she was almost out of breath. "Daddy, Daddy!" she cried. "Guess what? Guess what Uncle Dale told us at King's Kids!" (Dale Kauffman, the leader of the youth ministry, was universally known as "Uncle Dale.")

"I don't know, Misha," I said. "What did he tell you?"

"He said I have a *destiny!*" she beamed. "A destiny all my own, a special one from God that no one else has." My daughter rambled on and on about the destiny that Uncle Dale had told her she had, about how wonderful it was, about how not only Misha but *everyone* had a unique destiny given to them by God.

I thought, *Way to go, Uncle Dale. You really got through to them.* Eventually Misha calmed down a bit and snuggled next to me on the couch with her head resting on my shoulder. We sat there together, not talking, just enjoying the moment. After a while Misha raised her head and looked at me, her eyes wide, a serious look suddenly on her face. "Daddy?" she said.

"Yes, honey?"

"I just have one question."

"What's that?"

"Daddy—what's a destiny?"

I had to smile. My daughter was so excited about having a destiny, yet she wasn't sure what a destiny was! I suspect a lot of us are like that when it comes to the question of our true identity. We suspect we have one; we just don't know what it is. We may know in our heads that we are God's sons and daughters, adopted into his family, heirs to all the splendor and riches of his kingdom—but we're not always entirely clear on what all that *means*.

In the last chapter, we spoke at some length of the various mistaken identities that many of us carry. Now let's try to gain a clearer understanding of our true identity as a friend of God.

GOD DOESN'T MAKE MISTAKES

The first thing we must grasp about our true identity is that we were *planned and wanted by God*. There is not a single person alive who was not planned in the heart of God long before they came into being. Psalm 139 says it beautifully:

For thou didst form my inward parts,
thou didst knit me together in my mother's womb.

I praise thee, for thou art fearful and wonderful.
   Wonderful are thy works!
Thou knowest me right well;
   my frame was not hidden from thee,
when I was being made in secret,
   intricately wrought in the depths of the earth.
Thy eyes beheld my unformed substance;
   in thy book were written, every one of them,
the days that were formed for me,
   when as yet there was none of them.   Ps 139:13-16

What a wonderful, poetic description of the way God himself took part in designing us, shaping us, bringing us into being—even to the point of planning out his purposes for our lives in advance. (By the way, those verses go a long way toward answering my daughter's question, "What's a destiny?")

Maybe you are troubled by the fact that you were conceived by a mother and father who were not married—what is termed "illegitimate." Or perhaps your parents may have told you that you were "a mistake," that your parents hadn't wanted any more children and then you came along "by accident." Or you may never have even *met* one or both of your parents.

But in God's family, there are no illegitimate children, no "mistakes," no "accidents," no orphans. Certain *acts* may be illegitimate, but there are no illegitimate children to God. God wanted us. He planned us. The manner of our coming into this world may have fallen short of God's plan for our birth. Nevertheless, the fundamental truth remains unchanged: despite the sinfulness and weakness of our parents, the sovereign Lord called us into being. He planned our existence, even if our parents sinned during our conception. God is infinitely greater than the sins and shortcomings of earthly men and women.

I remember one time when I was a kid, watching my dad build a table. Now, my father's a great preacher. But while he may be masterful in proclaiming the good news, he's usually all thumbs when it comes to carpentry.

In the case of this particular table, Dad gathered up a bunch of stray pieces of lumber, grabbed a hammer and some nails, and went to it. When he was done, there were pieces of wood pointing off in all directions and nails sticking out all over the place. The table could barely stand up by itself, let alone support anything else.

The Bible tells us we are "[God's] workmanship, created in Christ Jesus" (Eph 2:10; see 2 Cor 5:17). When we hear that, a lot of us think of ourselves as being something like that table. We envision God standing around with a bunch of left-over parts, stuck with the job of somehow fashioning them into a human being. He does the best he can—which is pretty good, of course, since he *is* God, after all. But given what he has to work with, and given that he has so many other, higher, priorities—it's no wonder that we often feel we can barely stand up by ourselves, let alone be useful for anything else.

But it's not like that at all. I believe that God has sovereignly planned and arranged everything about us: our ancestry, our genetic code, our cultural heritage, our nationality, our personality, our life-shaping experiences—all with a view to fulfilling his master plan for our lives.

What an astonishing truth: with all our unique traits and qualities, all our strengths, all our limitations, the fact remains that *we are exactly the way God wanted us to be*. It's not as though someone came along and told God he had to create us, and that he would just have to do the best he could with the materials at hand. God was free to conceive of us in any way he wished. And, having done so, he had unlimited capacity to form and fashion us precisely according to his plan. God could even create new "raw material" to work with if he needed to!

The very same commitment in the heart of God that brings us into existence and shapes us also brings us into friendship with God. Our heavenly Father has adopted us as his children and made us his friends. He has given us a special destiny for our lives. As long as we are open to God and obedient to him, there is nothing that can keep him from loving us, and nothing that can prevent him from fulfilling his purpose in our lives.

A WHOLE NEW PERSON

A Christian is a person who has become someone he or she was not before. Becoming a Christian is not just getting something from God, no matter how great those things are, but becoming a brand new person.

This is not just a position we have been given, nor is it something we receive because of making right choices. When we receive Christ by faith into our hearts, we are no longer sinners, but children of God. We are loved, destined for heaven, adopted into God's family because we have been born again (see Jn 3:3-7).

You might be tempted to think, "I know that God sees me through the blood of Jesus and that I'm clothed with his righteousness." Granted, God forgives us and washes away our sin, but our heavenly Father does not just see you through the blood of Jesus. He sees *you!* He sees you as the unique special person he has created you to be, and he sees you as the new creation you have become. He sees your sins when you commit them. He sees your weaknesses and failures, but most important of all, he sees you as his child. He sees you through eyes of love.

David Needham compares our recreation in Christ to physical birth: "Being born isn't simply someone getting something more that one didn't have before (like getting the Holy Spirit). No! Being born is becoming *someone who was not there before*. And that is exactly the issue in spiritual new birth."[1]

We become a new person, a new creation, a spiritual person, through trusting in Christ's forgiveness. He forgives our sins, and makes us someone we never dreamed of becoming: a child of God.

What happens to us is not magic. God does not take something out of you and put something new in you, and presto, you are magically turned into a saint overnight. What does happen is that God by his Spirit comes to dwell in us. When this happens we experience the rebirth of our spirit. We still have our own character developed over many years. This new birth does not change our personality, nor does it take away all the consequences of past sins or problems, or change our character overnight. But when we become a new spiritual person, God enables us to deal with our character defects in a spiritual manner.

We also possess a free will. At any time we can go back to our old ways of dealing with sin and problems and temptations. But we can also choose to invoke what is now ours by virtue of being born again. God who dwells within us will enable us and help us overcome those problems, if we ask his help.

This ongoing process of confronting old habits and character weaknesses inevitably carries pain. It is not easy. Old habits die hard. But we develop strength of character as we face our weak points and problems. God uses the struggle to renew us and conform us to be like Jesus.

The Bible teaches that before our new birth we were "in Adam," the end result being death. Now we are in a new family; we are "in Christ" and the result is life (see 1 Cor

15:22). We have literally changed families. Our former family owned an inheritance of death, but as members of God's family we have a new inheritance to eagerly anticipate.

We all share a magnificent birthright! By understanding and accepting our identity as children of God, we can claim all that God has for us as his precious sons and daughters.

I pray that this astounding truth becomes more than words to you. If it does not, stop right now and ask God to reveal the wonder of this great truth to your heart and mind. As a believer in Christ, you belong to God! You are accepted as his child! You are in Christ! You are his friend!

GIVEN GIFTS BY MY FATHER IN HEAVEN

Not only did God create us in his image and recreate us to be in his family, but in doing so he planted within us *spiritual gifts* to enable us to serve him in accordance with his plan for our lives. I see tremendous confusion among Christians about spiritual gifts, and a lot could be said about them. I simply want to make the point that each and every one of us has been gifted, in any number of ways, to be of service to the Lord.

Spiritual gifts are not just for the celebrities, for the so-called "spiritual superstars." The Bible does not say, "Well done, thou good and famous servant." God gives spiritual gifts to every single person. Upon the moment of our conception, these gifts are deposited deep within our being, unique treasures that will enable us to have a ministry of service in God's kingdom.

What kind of gifts do I mean? For some it might be the gift of giving—the ability to make money that can be invested in God's work. It might be the gift of hospitality, or encouragement, or administration. I think that one of the church's main tasks is to help each Christian discern his or her specific gifts, and to affirm every individual in the ministry for which those gifts equip them.

God wants each one of us—with our unique personal history and heritage, our unique talents, and our own special gifts—to be able to maintain a sense of his purpose in the world, and to understand the way our particular attributes equip us to be a part of it.

I don't mean going off on a complicated personal quest for meaning. Rather, as we grow more confident of the fact that we are God's friends, he is able to reveal to us more and more about his purposes and about our role in helping to accomplish them. And we don't have to *search* for our gifts. As we just *serve* people, those unique gifts will naturally emerge.

We've been talking about the fact that we have each been planned, designed, and created by God, and especially equipped by him for his service. If that tremendous truth really sunk in, it would dramatically revolutionize our lives. But I'll take it even one step further: I believe that each of us is *a work of art* in God's eyes.

LOVED WITHOUT LIMITS

A fourth aspect of our true identity is that we are the recipients of God's love *without boundaries or limitations*. Do you realize there is absolutely *nothing* you could ever do to make God stop loving you? You can never do anything that would cause him to stop desiring an intimate relationship with you.

Most of us know from painful personal experience how easy it is for human friends to fail us, to lose interest in us, to reject us. But God is not like that. He is *faithful*. God will pursue us to the ends of the earth, even into the deepest pits of sin, to bring us into fellowship with himself. We are *loved*.

One day, a colleague of mine, John Goodfellow, was sitting in a bar in Amsterdam, Holland, where we lived at the time. He sensed the Lord calling his attention to a particular man seated at the other end of the bar. The Lord seemed to speak to him: "Go witness to that man."

John felt understandably awkward about approaching a complete stranger in a bar, so he hesitated briefly. The voice came again: "Go talk to him. Tell him there's nothing he can do to make me stop loving him."

My friend sat silently, pondering his options. Finally he said, "Lord, you know I want to do whatever you ask of me. It's just that with this one, I'd like to be sure it really is you. I'll tell you what: if it's really *your* will that I go witness to that man, cause the music here in the bar to stop."

No sooner had John said these words than the jukebox broke down. So he drew a deep breath, got up from his table, and walked to the end of the bar.

"I know we don't know each other," John began. "We've never met before. And I know this is probably going to sound crazy, but—well, I think God wants me to tell you that there's nothing you could ever do to make him stop loving you."

The man just stared at him for a moment. "Do you know who I am?" he asked.

"No," John said. "I've never seen you before."

"I'm the high priest in a Satanist church," the man said.

You can imagine John's shock! We lived two doors down from that "church," located in Amsterdam's red-light district. We knew it was there. We had both walked past it hundreds of times and knew how evil it was. But God still loved those people. He longed to reach out to them, to offer them friendship with himself. That's how utterly dedicated God is to each and every person he has created!

By the way, this incident provoked us to pray for this particular man and his "co-workers." Several of the people involved in that occult group were wonderfully converted during our time in Holland!

Let me summarize the true nature of who we are this way: we are created *by* God for friendship *with* God. These two great truths proclaim *who* we are. The first point about our true identity is that we are planned and wanted by God. The second follows from the first: God so deeply longed for us to enjoy friendship with him that he made the ultimate sacrifice in order to make that friendship possible. He then brought us into his own family by adoption to insure our relationship.

This is what God has done *for* us. But what has he done *in* us? That is the third aspect of our true identity. We have said that our true identity is found in the fact that we are created by God—planned and wanted by God—and that we are pardoned by God through the ultimate sacrifice, the death of his Son Jesus on the cross. As God's friends, we are also the dwelling place of God.

Late one night, Jesus was approached by a man named Nicodemus. This Jewish teacher of the law of God was struggling to gain a clearer understanding of who Jesus was and of what his message meant. Jesus simply said to Nicodemus, "Truly, truly, I say to you, unless one is born anew [or born from above], he cannot see the kingdom of God" (Jn 3:3).

Jesus was saying that because of what he had done for us on the cross, we could have new life: the Holy Spirit of God would come to dwell within us. How much more intimate a relationship with God could we possibly have than to have him actually take up residence within us? And yet that is precisely what he does. The Bible says that we are the dwelling place of God.

This theme—that we have new life in God through Jesus' sacrifice on the cross and through the Holy Spirit coming to dwell within us—is echoed throughout the pages of Scripture:

But God, who is rich in mercy, out of the great love with which he loved us, even when we were dead through our trespasses, made us alive together with Christ.... **Eph 2:4-5**

And you, who were dead in trespasses and the uncircumcision of your flesh, God made alive together with him....

Col 2:13

Therefore, if any one is in Christ, he is a new creation; the old has passed away, behold, the new has come. **2 Cor 5:17**

Note the expression "in Christ" in that last passage. Paul uses that expression more than one hundred sixty times in his letters. This particular phrase speaks of a profound mutuality of intimacy in our relationship with God. Jesus is in us; we are in him. Our life is no longer simply "ours," it is also *his* in a deep and abiding way.

As Paul put it so dramatically: "I have been crucified with Christ; it is no longer I who live, but Christ who lives in me; and the life I now live in the flesh I live by faith in the Son of God, who loved me and gave himself for me" (Gal 2:20).

It is no longer I who live, but Christ who lives in me. That, in a nutshell, is the message of friendship with God: that he himself comes to dwell in us!

How, then, do we grow in intimacy with God? By working harder? By giving more? By reading longer portions of Scripture? No! It is by resting in our newfound relationship as a friend of God. As we understand and accept our true identity as God's friends, we are free to get better acquainted with the one who dwells in our hearts.

We do not know God as a friend by burning ourselves out in religious activity, or even in service to God's kingdom. We know his friendship by receiving and enjoying the gift he offers us, the gift of himself, living within us.

"MAN'S BEST FRIEND"

Not long ago my family acquired a new member: a little eight-week-old Labrador puppy named Mack. He is cute and cuddly and utterly fascinating to me. Every morning about six or six thirty I come downstairs and put food in his dog dish. Now, bear in mind that this rapidly growing puppy has been sleeping for almost eight to ten hours, and has had nothing to eat for even longer than that.

But what does Mack do? He sniffs the food, maybe takes a single bite, then runs across the room and jumps up into my lap. I pet him and hug him and scratch him by the ears, and Mack whimpers and groans the most delightful sighs of affection. He wants companionship even more than he wants food! I have never seen a dog so hungry for love!

If only we Christians could learn to be the same way in our relationship with God. If only we could recognize that he desires nothing more than for us to draw near to him, to be close to him, to enjoy the intimacy he has given us as his gift!

Christianity is not about rules, or principles, or philosophical propositions. It is about a *person*, and the relationship we can have with that person. In his book, *Growing in Grace*, Bob George sums it up wonderfully:

In contrast to religions of the world which offer mankind "ten steps to spiritual fulfillment," or "the nine-fold path to enlightenment," Jesus Christ continues to say, "Come to me." He says, "I am the bread of life; he who comes to me will never go hungry, and he who believes in me will never be thirsty" (Jn 6:35). "I am the light of the world; whoever follows me will never be in darkness, but will have the light of life" (Jn 8:12). "I am the gate; whoever enters through me will be saved. He will come in and go out and find pasture" (Jn 10:9). "I am the good shepherd. The good shepherd lays down his life for the sheep. I give them eternal life and they shall never perish" (Jn 10:11, 28). "I am the way, the truth, and the life; no one comes to the Father except through me" (Jn 14:6). "I am the vine, you are the branches. If a man remains in me and I in him, he will bear much fruit" (Jn 15:5). "I am the resurrection and the life; he who believes in me shall live" (Jn 11:25-26).

Jesus Christ did not come to *show us* the way, he *is* the way. He did not just teach us some truth, he *is* the truth. He did not just leave us a manual to live by; he *is* our life.[2]

Notice that all these passages start with the words, "I am." These are only a few of the places where Jesus tells us who he is and what he is like—where he reveals his true identity to us.

The Bible also has a great deal to say about *our* true identity. I'd like to close this chapter with another set of "I am" statements, this time referring to ourselves as we now exist in God's eyes. The next time you're tempted to slip into thinking of yourself according to a false identity, you might look over this list, look up some of these Scripture passages, and remind yourself of who you really are.

I am...

1. I am a *child* of God (Rom 8:16).
2. I am *redeemed* from the hand of the enemy (Ps 107:2).
3. I am *forgiven* (Col 1:13, 14).
4. I am *saved* by grace through faith (Eph 2:8).
5. I am *justified* (Rom 5:1).

6. I am *sanctified* (1 Cor 5:17).

7. I am a *new creation* (2 Cor 5:17).

8. I am a *partaker* of his divine nature (2 Pt 1:4).

9. I am *redeemed* from the curse of the law (Gal 3:13).

10. I am *delivered* from the powers of darkness (Col 1:13).

11. I am *led* by the Spirit of God (Rom 8:14).

12. I am a *son or daughter* of God (Rom 8:14).

13. I am *kept* under his wings wherever I go (Ps 91:11).

14. I am *cared for* by Jesus (1 Pt 5:7).

15. I am *strong* in the Lord and in the power of his might (Eph 6:10).

16. I am *able* to do all things through Christ who strengthens me (Phil 4:13).

17. I am an *heir* of God and a *joint heir* with Jesus (Rom 8:17).

18. I am *empowered* to do all the Lord's commandments (Dt 28:12).

19. I am *blessed* in my coming in and my going out (Dt 28:6).

20. I am *blessed* with all spiritual blessings (Eph 1:3).

21. I am *saved* by Jesus' wounds (1 Pt 2:24).

22. I am more than a *conqueror* (Rom 8:37).

23. I am an *overcomer* by the blood of the Lamb and by the word of my testimony (Rv 12:11).

24. I am *empowered* to cast down vain imaginations (2 Cor 10:4-5).

25. I am *able* to bring every thought into captivity (2 Cor 10:5).

26. I am being *transformed* by the renewing of my mind (Rom 12:1, 2).

27. I am a *co-laborer* together with God (1 Cor 5:21).

28. I am *a friend of God* (Jn 15:15).

7

Nine Barriers to Friendship with God

MY WIFE AND I LIVED OVERSEAS for twenty-one years. One of the striking things about being so immersed in a foreign country is noticing the way Western entertainment infiltrates popular culture. The clothes people wear, the hairstyles they adopt, even the slang expressions they use, often can be traced back to a well-known rock singer, TV actor, or some movie star.

A few years ago, for example, I noticed that everyone suddenly began using the phrase, "Go ahead, make my day," immortalized by tough cop Clint Eastwood. Another popular expression was "I'm going to make him an offer he can't refuse," employed by Marlon Brando in *The Godfather*.

"The Don" would work behind the scenes, manipulating circumstances and orchestrating events, until he had maneuvered the other party into a situation where the thing he wanted them to do was the only thing they *could* do. It became an offer they *literally* couldn't refuse. Of course, the reason why the individual couldn't refuse was that if he did, the Godfather would arrange to have his brains blown out.

God the Father doesn't operate that way. Still, at first glance, it might seem that God's offer of friendship would also be an offer that no one in his right mind would decline. I mean, who wouldn't want to be "on the in" with the Master of the Universe? Who wouldn't jump at the chance to enjoy that freedom of access, that intimacy? Especially if it came as a gift?

But a great many people do not, in fact, accept God's offer of intimacy. Or if they do, they give up on God when serious difficulties come along.

Every family goes through hard times. It is particularly during those times of testing and difficulty that we grow into our destiny. Our inheritance as God's children brings with it testing. Scripture tells us that God even arranges problematic circumstances to teach us and prepare us for his special plan and purpose for our life. Even those difficulties brought against us by the enemy are allowed by God for our testing and refining.

God employs the negative experiences in our lives—even the ways other people deliberately try to harm us—and makes them work for our good and for the fulfillment of his plan.

This foundation-building is such a crucial concept that we will discuss it at length in chapter ten. For now, the important point to underline is that even the things other people intend for evil, God can use for the good. As we grow in friendship with him, our ability to trust in his love for us even in the midst of trouble will grow ever deeper and stronger.

In this chapter, we'll take a look at some of the more common barriers to friendship that can stand between us and God—and how they can be surmounted. Whatever the barrier may be that has come between you and God, *trust him*. Don't let anything or anyone come between you and our loving Father.

THE SIN BARRIER

The first barrier to intimacy with God is familiar to us under a variety of different names. The humanists call it "human weakness." The New Agers call it a "lack of self-actualization." Psychologists call it "abnormal behavior." Many people nowadays blame it on being "dysfunctional." But the Bible calls it *sin*.

The book of Genesis records the story of Adam and Eve's tragic choice in the garden, and of the terrible consequences that followed. In the beginning, the first man and woman were created in friendship with God. But Adam and Eve listened to the voice of the serpent and disobeyed God. In trying to reach and grasp for more, they in effect rejected divine friendship. Satan sowed the deadly seeds of temptation in their hearts that eventually bore the fruit of rebellion.

Adam and Eve no longer recognized God's law—the one against eating the fruit of the tree in the middle of the garden—as a wise and loving limitation, but as an unreasonable prohibition. Their choice was simple. They could decide to trust God—the one who had created the beautiful world around them, who had created them to reign over it as his son and daughter, who had given them the gift of intimacy with himself—or they could decide not to trust him.

In the end, Adam and Eve chose not to trust God. They refused to accept the limitations of their humanity. They decided, as so many of us decide so often, to try to "have their cake and eat it, too."

Adam and Eve wanted to retain their position in the garden, but they also wanted to rise above that position. They wanted to be like God. But in trying to become like God, they not only failed to become *more* than they were, they actually became *less* than they were. Not only did they fail to achieve the glory that belongs to God alone, but they forfeited the special glory that he had granted the human race.

The Bible tells us that each and every one of us—you and me included—have ratified the original sin of our first parents. In his letter to the Romans, Paul writes, "Therefore... sin came into the world through one man and death through sin, and so death spread to all men *because all men sinned*" (Rom 5:12, emphasis mine).

Adam and Eve's fall was a cataclysmic event for humankind. Not only did they lose their relationship with God, but their sin affected the entire human race. We lost our physical perfection: the very fact that we get older, that we experience the aches and pains of the aging process, serves as an almost daily reminder.

We also no longer have the same creative abilities as Adam and Eve. The occasional emergence of a Michelangelo or an Einstein only gives us a glimpse of how far we have fallen. We lost much more—our emotional perfection, our relational perfection, our spiritual perfection.

Most tragically of all, we suffered a great loss in our capacity to give of ourselves to others, which is the very essence of love. Our selfishness is the greatest barrier of all to friendship with God. It is not so much that we have made a single, once-for-all choice to ratify Adam and Eve's rebellion, but that we continually make innumerable choices of selfishness, insincerity, greed, lust, dishonesty, pride—the list goes on and on.

We see it from the earliest days of human life. When we first come into the world as crying infants, we quickly learn that we can usually get our own way by fussing. From the very beginning, our will becomes entrenched in self-fulfillment and self-gratification.

One old saying goes: "Sow a thought, reap a choice; sow a choice, reap a habit; sow a habit, reap a character; sow a character, reap a destiny." That's exactly what all of us do throughout our lives, day by day. By consistently sowing selfish thoughts and actions, we become selfish, and in the end we reap separation from God.

We are sinners, the Bible teaches us, *because we sin*. Ephesians 2:1-4 says that we are by nature sinful because of the trespasses we commit against God and his laws. When we follow our selfish desires we become "children of wrath." We reap a character because we ratify the original sin of Adam and Eve. Or as it says in the book of Isaiah, "All we like sheep have gone astray; *we have turned every one to his own way...*" (Is 53:6, emphasis mine).

One of the painful byproducts of our sin is our ongoing struggle to find meaning without God. We go our own way, like dumb sheep, searching in religion, self-improvement classes, psychic healers, sex, pleasure, materialism, achievement at work, and many other ways to find who we are. We seek to find our identity outside the only source of meaning for our lives: relationship with our loving God.

Our sin leads us to endlessly search, trying to cope without God. But all we ever find in the end are bigger barriers. Great walls separate us from the only one who loves us without condition or measure.

SINNED AGAINST

Sin is a barrier to friendship with God in another way as well: not only does our own sin stand in the way, but the sins that others have committed *against* us stand in the way as well. We are not only sinners but also sinned-against, not only perpetrators but also victims—often the victims of other victims.

I learned a lot about this during our years in Amsterdam. The capital of Holland is notorious for its sexual license, and our ministry headquarters were right in the middle of the red-light district. We were able to observe at close range the dynamics of sin and victimization in their most unvarnished form.

Several classes of prostitutes worked these streets. We actually used to see some of them dropped off for work in the evenings by their husbands or boyfriends driving Mercedes-Benzes. The women would work their eight hours, make twelve to fourteen hundred dollars and then go home. They wore mink coats and vacationed in the Caribbean.

But the majority of these prostitutes had come from tragic, nightmarish circumstances. Nowadays we talk a lot about "dysfunctional" backgrounds, but that kind of clinical terminology doesn't even begin to do justice to the reality of their horror. These victims had experienced rejection and abuse as a way of life. One young woman who became involved with our ministry said to me, "Why not? My uncle used to do it to me for free. Why shouldn't I make them pay me now?" Steeped in bitterness over having been molested by her uncle, she continued to express her hate and anger by working as a prostitute and taking out her revenge on any male who crossed her path. And these prostitutes who had been so shamefully used all their lives, were now being used by the little old ladies who rented rooms to them. Seemingly sweet, grandmotherly ladies, charged one hundred fifty dollars for an eight-hour shift. They rented out rooms three shifts a day, seven days a week, growing rich off the bondage of others!

Most of the women were addicted to drugs and had gotten into prostitution to support their habit. Many times we would get close enough to one of these victims that she would begin, oh-so-cautiously, to open up to us. But facing the painful reality of her emotional wounds would become so overwhelming that she soon would run away, back into the horrific world of prostitution and drugs.

The tragedy of their lives was more extreme than what has happened to most of us. Yet all of us have been victimized by others' sin in one way or another. We have all been hurt and rejected by others; we have all built up walls and put on masks to protect ourselves from being hurt again; we have all chased down blind alleys in our search for escape. Being sinned against undermines our relationships with others, and it certainly undermines our relationship with God.

BURIED UNDER GUILT

We are often afflicted, as well, by the burden of *false guilt* heaped upon us by others. I'm not talking now about what might be called "legitimate" guilt, the kind that is rightly ours when we have actually done something wrong. I mean the false-guilt that is heaped upon us when we are put down by others, told that we are not doing enough to please God, told that we have failed him in more ways than we can even count. When this happens, we are driven by a deep sense of condemnation that keeps us from believing that God loves us.

The primary way we develop our conscience is by internalizing the standards of people we consider important in our lives. We want them to approve of us, so we incorporate their values and make them our own. When this dynamic works properly, it is what the Bible refers to as bringing up children in the discipline of the Lord. Indeed, such a passing on of values is the basis of the Christian home, the foundation of Christian education, Sunday school, youth groups, and so on.

When the standards that are internalized are founded in Scripture, rooted in loving relationships, and reinforced by consistent godly example, the result will be a healthy Christian conscience. But this process designed by God can work the other way, too. If wrongly applied, it results in a damaged, overly-sensitive conscience that can plague us with an overwhelming sense of failure and condemnation.

I have seen such damage where there is an excessive emphasis on minor rules and regulations within a family or church, or
when the punishment for breaking the rules is disproportion-
ate to their importance. Legalistic, grace-less homes and
churches tend to produce warped consciences that entrap
Christians in guilt.

This burden of guilt poses a major barrier that prevents
people from truly believing that God wants to be their friend.
They are perpetually plagued by the nagging sense that God
couldn't love them, *couldn't* want them for a friend—they
haven't done enough to earn his favor. Unfortunately, preach-
ers and evangelists often discover that they can use this guilt to
manipulate and control people. They can even unwittingly
engage in a kind of spiritual blackmail that eventually destroys
people's ability to trust in God's love for them.

I think of a young man named Sonny, filled with a wonderful zest for life and a passion for fun. He loved to hunt and fish
and do things with other people. But at the same time, Sonny
was one of the most guilt-ridden people I have ever known.
He had been raised by a strict aunt who constantly made him
feel condemned. He could never do enough, and what he did
do was never *good* enough. This aunt was a victim herself, having been abused by her husband. Unfortunately, she took out
her pain and guilt and shame on Sonny.

The best word to describe Sonny was "driven." He came to
church for all the meetings: Sunday morning worship, Sunday
evening worship, Wednesday night prayer meeting, Friday
night youth group. He answered the altar call every Sunday
night, trying desperately to get right with God, trying to figure out what more he could do to be acceptable in God's
sight.

In the end this drivenness got the best of Sonny and he
took his own life. His short life was filled with self-flagellation
and a search for acceptance, but he never could live up to

everything that was expected of him. He could never satisfy the unreasonable demands of his malformed conscience, never overcome the barrier of false-guilt that lay between him and an experience of friendship with God.

TOXIC FAITH

Sonny's story points toward the fourth barrier to friendship with God: *religion*. Religion, as I am using the term, focuses on *outward* forms rather than *inward* attitudes. It is more concerned with duties than with the condition of our hearts, more concerned with obeying rules than with pursuing a relationship. Religiosity judges people by what they do or by what they don't do, whereas God judges the heart. One of the greatest enemies of grace is the complex web of religious substitutes we manufacture to take the place of relationship with God. It is a toxic faith that kills spiritual life.

One of the most striking statements in the entire Bible occurs in Paul's letter to the Galatians, in which he accuses those believers of having deserted the faith. It is the same expression one would use of a soldier who has gone into battle, and then not only turned his back on his comrades but actually gone over to the other side. Paul said the Galatians had "deserted him who called you" and had actually "turned to a different gospel" (see Gal 1:6).

What was this different gospel? It was a gospel of religion. Later in this same letter, Paul upbraids the Galatians: "Are you so foolish? Having begun with the Spirit, are you now ending with the flesh?" (Gal 3:3). By "flesh," Paul means the religious system of rules and regulations that characterized Judaism— what I am referring to as religion.

Religion is a substitute for relationship with God. It lives on our reluctance to acknowledge our utter dependence on God and on Jesus' work upon the cross. Instead of humility and surrender, we search for ways to build a righteousness based on our own good deeds. This kind of religion is "a *form* of godliness that denies the power of God" (see 2 Tm 3:5). It can be an insurmountable barrier to true friendship with God, which is built on humble acceptance of what God has done for us.

But the wonderful truth is that God's grace *can* break through the hard shell of religion. I remember a man who pastored a small church many years ago. It happened that the daughter of one of the deacons and the son of one of the elders fell in love. It also happened that they got pregnant.

Just teenagers at the time, they were frightened and ashamed, and more than a little bitter toward the church, which they had experienced as legalistic and condemning. So they ran away. This pair had no money, of course, and the boy wasn't able to find a steady job. They ended up living in a flophouse motel on the bad side of town.

The pastor, even though he was in a church that majored in law, was himself a man of grace. He made up his mind that he was going to bring those two young people back. After several weeks of searching, he tracked them down to the seedy hotel where they were staying. It took a lot longer to persuade them to come back to the church. They wanted nothing to do with its rigidity and harshness.

But in the end the pastor prevailed. He called a special meeting of the church. The whole congregation of about one hundred fifty people showed up—curious, of course, as sinful human nature is inclined to be, but also concerned for the two families involved.

The pastor brought the young couple to the front of the church. You could see the fear and resentment written on their faces, mixed in with the trepidation and embarrassment. But the pastor stood beside them, and spoke of the return of the prodigal son. He spoke about the prodigal's father, who welcomed back his errant son with open arms. And he spoke about the prodigal's brother, who had nothing but scorn and derision for his sibling. It wasn't hard to see which attitude he hoped the church would adopt.

"These are God's children," the pastor said, "and God is prepared to forgive them and welcome them back into his family. But they are also *our* children. They belong to all of us. We are their earthly family. And now it is time for us to welcome them back, too. No bitterness. No shaming. No recriminations. Just forgiveness, and acceptance, and love."

One person in the congregation came forward, then a second, and then a third. This trickle soon grew into a rush of people making their way to the front, reaching out to the young couple, hugging them, tearfully welcoming them back. Before long the young man and woman were weeping, too, unable to withstand the outpouring of affection. They were restored to fellowship with the church and, more important, to friendship with God.

I heard this true story from the young man himself, now married to his teenage sweetheart and the father of several children. *He is now the pastor of that very church.*

THE BOOTSTRAP MENTALITY

Another barrier to friendship with God is what is often called "individualism." I call it *self-reliance*. Who among us hasn't grown up listening to the stories of the pioneers who hacked their way across the wilderness to forge a new nation? Or the rags-to-riches stories of immigrants who came to the new world from overseas and conquered the odds by "making it big" in America? They literally pulled themselves up by their own bootstraps.

I once wrote that individualism is as American as hotdogs, baseball, apple pie, and motherhood. Indeed, Americans cherish as sacred their right to "life, liberty, and the pursuit of happiness." For individualistic Americans, anything that stands between them and thinking for themselves, working for themselves, living for themselves, and voting for themselves, is seen as sacreligious, a violation of their most basic rights.[1]

But if this pioneering spirit is not submitted to the lordship of Jesus Christ, it can turn people into egomaniacs who have no room in their hearts for anyone but themselves. When individualism is divorced from moral foundations and planted in the fertile soil of a hedonistic culture, it ultimately produces a way of life that is neither beneficial to us as individuals nor healthy for society as a whole.

Self-reliance is a great barrier to friendship with God. In fact, it is virtually the direct opposite of a personal relationship based on *God*-reliance. Even many Christians fall into the common trap of trying to work out their own problems in their own time and way, according to what *they* decide is right for *them*.

I find remarkable how many Christian books and tapes and radio programs use the *vocabulary* of faith when all they're really talking about is self-fulfillment. The message is no different from what you might find on the psychology shelf of your local paperback bookstore. Faith soon becomes just another tool for self-development, just another avenue to self-actualization.

Many people mistake self-discipline for pleasing God. They strive to do what is right, but for the wrong reasons. They are driven to pray longer and read the Bible more by feelings of guilt than by true love of God. They impose on their internal urges a stiff rigidity to always do what is "right," but such perfectionism does not come out of an understanding of their true identity as a child of God. They are driven to do what is right more by fear and a feeling of obligation.

I do not argue the fact that there is a place for spiritual disciplines. But when we are set free from searching and striving for more of God, and come to know who we truly are, these practices flow more effortlessly as a love-response to our new-found Father in heaven. Godly spiritual discipline is motivated by love, and is characterized by a deep sense of well-being, of belonging to God.

But if the Bible is true, then our fallen, sinful self is the *last* thing we want to develop, fulfill, or discipline. The message of the gospel is not that we can finally figure out how to find meaning in life or improve ourselves "once and for all," but that we can step down and let Jesus take his rightful place as the center of our lives. Only when we have done this can we enjoy the intimacy with God that he intends for us, an intimacy that comes from true friendship with God. Pulling ourselves up by our own bootstraps will never bring us closer to God.

THE CHASM OF CYNICISM

A *cynic* is a person who believes that the actions of others are always motivated by selfishness. Cynics don't believe it's *possible* for someone to act selflessly; they're always thinking, "What's their angle? What's in it for them?" He or she tends to be pessimistic, derisive, mocking, and sarcastic. Such a person exhibits a habitual disposition to look on the dark side of everything. For the cynic, every silver lining has a cloud! These folks tend to especially mistrust professions of faith, particularly by public leaders.

In case you can't already tell, cynics are not pleasant people to be around! Unfortunately, they are seldom content just to be cynical themselves; they invariably go around trying to undermine the confidence of other people in the objects of their own cynicism. Often they have been offended by someone or have felt betrayed at some point in their lives. Cynics often tend to visit their disillusionment upon others. A group under the influence of a cynic is given to suspicion, backbiting, divisiveness, and judgmentalism.

In many cases, people slip into cynicism as a way of hiding from their own failures and shortcomings. Acting "above it all" can be a way of protecting themselves from acknowledging that they, too, have faults. As long as they can pass judgment on others, cynics feel relieved of the responsibility to pass judgment on themselves. In this sense, we can recognize cynicism as a form of pride. Only the proud elevate themselves above others and then look down their noses at the whole world, unable to see that they are guilty of the same faults they deride in others.

Before we can be free of cynical attitudes, we have to acknowledge that we ourselves are guilty of the things we condemn in others. Cynicism must be confronted in a spirit of humility, acknowledging our own weaknesses and faults before God, realizing that he alone is the appropriate one to take responsibility for the failings of others.

Once we realize that God is big enough to accept others with their limitations, then we realize that he is big enough to accept us with *our* limitations as well. That is the point at which we are able to accept God's offer of intimate friendship with himself.

BRICK WALLS OF PERFECTION

Perfectionism is another common obstacle to friendship with God. This approach to life displays four main characteristics. The first, of course, is the drive to make everything in our lives proceed flawlessly. But along with that doomed desire inevitably comes the need to find scapegoats when things *don't* proceed flawlessly. The end result can be a cruel distortion of priorities and values that makes intimacy with God—or with anyone else for that matter—almost impossible.

Perfectionists engage in a relentless effort to prove themselves superior. It is their way of feeling important, of feeling special. Western culture especially places a premium on accomplishment and achievement. Technological confidence that everything can be broken down into a step-by-step process can fill us with a sense of "oughtness." We ought to do this, we ought to have that, we ought to be this kind of person. People driven by perfection keep setting unreachable goals, and then strive with all their energy to attain them. Only then, they believe, will they be acceptable in the eyes of others.

Naturally, such a person inevitably falls short of the perfection they seek. This usually produces deep frustration and inner hostility toward life, toward "the world," toward other people, even toward God. The perfectionist who lives in this "treadmill bondage" goes through life angry. Everything and everybody seems unfair.

Perfectionists live with a strange combination of pride and low self-esteem that drives them onward toward their elusive goal of perfection, and also drives them away from meaningful relationships with others. They must always get the house cleaner, lose more weight, study more hours, push harder in sports—be more, do more, accomplish more, control everything and everyone around them, until they either alienate or simply ignore everyone in their life.

As pleased as they might like to be with their achievements, those striving for perfection find it impossible to accept praise or congratulations from others. The flaw seems obvious; the heights still unattained cast too dark a shadow. The engines of hurt, humiliation, fear, and resentment mercilessly drive them day after day, only to be boosted in power when measured against their seemingly puny efforts toward pleasing God or others.

Typically, low self-esteem increases in intensity in proportion to their quest for perfection. As it begins to eat away at perfectionists from the inside, they often go through life despising themselves, even seeking to destroy themselves. A temporary sense of relief may be sought through alcohol, drugs, excessive sexual behavior, religious extremism, or serious eating disorders.

How can this barrier of perfection be overcome? Can any escape route be forged from this treadmill of inner torment? Instead of trying to master life on their own strength, perfectionists need to grasp the liberating truth that God has offered them friendship with himself *just as they are*. Only that recognition can set them free from the drive to prove themselves, to earn the approval of God and others.

I once worked closely with a perfectionist, a man who had labored for years in full-time Christian ministry. This man was truly a genius. People always came to him when their cars or stereos or toasters broke down, because he could fix anything. His room was always immaculate. His clothes were always pressed. Even his beard was always neatly trimmed, daily in fact. If there was ever a guy who "had it all together," it was him.

And yet, in rare moments of honesty, he would admit that he almost always felt very far from God. Sometimes he covered over his nagging sense of distance from the Lord with his prodigious spiritual accomplishments. When he had been doing a good job of keeping up with his daily Bible study and his daily prayer time, when he had put extra hours into his ministry work, he felt on top of the world. But on other days, when he had not been able to keep up with all these things, he felt like a miserable failure.

I can still remember the night when the revelation finally pierced his heart that God's love for him was a gift, an expression of pure grace, not something he had to earn or deserve. For years, this man had been taught that the way to attain "Christian maturity" was to keep working, keep pressing on, keep striving. Now, he suddenly realized that the main thing he needed to do was simply to receive God's grace. When he was finally able to break through and accept God's gift of love, a revolutionary change began in his life.

THE GREED BARRIER

The 1988 hit movie, *Wall Street*, featured a financial tycoon named Gordon Gekko. At one point in the film, Gekko delivers a speech to a group of young investment bankers. He concludes by earnestly proclaiming, "Greed is good. Greed is right. Greed clarifies. It cuts through and captures the essence of the evolutionary spirit. Greed—mark my words—will save the U.S.A."

You could hardly ask for it to be stated more baldly. Give Gordon Gekko credit: what other people call by a variety of euphemisms—attaining a more satisfying lifestyle, reaching for success, the spirit of the eighties—he calls by its correct, biblical name. It is *greed*.

Far from saving us, greed will prove to be the undoing of any society—or any individual—that sells out to it. It has given us the so-called American rat-race, which I define as people buying things they don't need, with money they don't have, in order to keep up with people they don't like! Greed is terribly destructive of relationships because it distracts our attention from others to ourselves, and turns our energies from *giving* to *getting*.

Greed is part and parcel of our way of life as a nation. Yet the greatest consequence may not be that it turns someone into a greedy person. I believe the damage is more indirect, more insidious. Greed often requires compromise, commitments we must make in life just to stay afloat financially. The second job, the longer work hours, the unneeded expenditures all combine to exert unbelievable pressure on us. As a result, we can lose control of our lives.

If we allow ourselves to be driven by the unbridled desire to have the best, the newest, the most advanced, the most fashionable, we become a slave to the spirit of the age. We encumber ourselves with debts that demand we work harder and longer. We run ourselves ragged, leaving no time or energy for our spouses, our children, our friends, or ourselves. And worst of all, we end up squeezing God out of our schedule. Or if we do spend time with him, we come into his presence burdened with the frantic feelings of our busy, go, go, go lifestyle.

BREAKING THROUGH TO BROKENNESS

The last barrier to friendship with God that I will mention here is *lack of brokenness*. What God wants from us is not money, nor activity, nor time. What he desires from us more than anything else is what the Bible calls "a broken and contrite heart." King David expressed it so poignantly after he had been confronted with his sin of adultery with Bathsheba:

Create in me a clean heart, O God,
    and put a new and right spirit within me....
For thou hast no delight in sacrifice;
    were I to give a burnt offering,
thou wouldst not be pleased.
The sacrifice acceptable to God is a broken spirit;

a broken and contrite heart, O God, thou wilt not despise.

Ps 51:10, 16-17, emphasis mine

What does it mean to have a broken and contrite heart? It means that we see our selfishness and our sin as God sees them. That we experience godly sorrow over the greed and lust and pride that we have allowed to grow in our hearts, those inner attitudes which separate us from the wonderful gift of friendship that God offers us. It means that we call our defense mechanisms just that: barriers we hide behind. It also means we are honest about all our human efforts to cope as a Christian, rather than growing in a deep, abiding friendship with God.

Hudson Taylor found such a friendship with God. Even though he was converted at the age of fifteen and later served as a missionary to China, Taylor often expressed frustration over his failure to overcome sin. "He complained of coldness, love of pleasure, self-indulgence, and lack of excitement over personal Bible study and prayer."[2]

By 1869, Taylor's missionary work in China was proving successful. More workers were joining the effort; God was providing necessary finance. Still, Taylor struggled for a closer walk with God. Here was one of the giants of the Christian faith, involved in great exploits... and yet inwardly not satisfied in his relationship with the Lord.

Taylor's own words reflect his ongoing agony: "I prayed, agonized, fasted, strove, made resolutions, read the word more diligently, sought more time for retirement and meditation—but all was without effect. I knew that if I could abide in Christ all would be well, but I could not.... All the time I felt assured that there was in Christ all that I needed, but the practical question was how to get it out."[3]

Taylor reached a turning point in his life when he received a letter from a colleague. This simple message unlocked the door: *that friendship with God came not from striving after faith, but resting in the faithful one.*

But what does that mean?

Taylor came to believe that his job was simply to focus his life on Jesus. And that as he did so, all of the resources that are in Christ would be availabe to him as well. This missionary giant recognized that only when *his* barriers came down and when *his* striving stopped, and when he then embraced and cultivated a brokenness of spirit would he receive the power and life of Christ.

Our responsibility is to recognize and confess to God the barriers to our friendship as they are revealed to us. The "revealing" may come through the Holy Spirit speaking to our hearts, or it may come through times of testing which reveal our own weaknesses and need of God.

Just as Joseph learned to see God at work in the rejection and betrayal of his brothers, the temptation of Potipher's wife, the isolation of prison, and the broken promises of the baker and the butler, so we must cry out to God for eyes to see what he is doing in our lives. We must implore him to release the treasures that are within us in Christ, and enable us to respond as God would have us respond.

As we cultivate this contrite spirit, as we daily choose to be yielded to God in every circumstance of life, as we humble ourselves before God and others each time we have responded in a willful, proud, unteachable way, then we are able to receive that which belongs to us by birthright. We are the children of God, and Christ is in us. Let us allow Christ to control us, to manifest himself through us.

A broken and contrite heart is a humble heart. It is ready to acknowledge its own sin. It is ready to forgive the sin of others. It is ready to reject self-righteous religious striving, self-centered individualism, self-glorifying cynicism, self-defeating perfectionism, self-serving greed. It is ready to acknowledge

God for who he is, and to simply and humbly accept the gift of intimacy that he offers.

Can I encourage you to do some honest reflection right now? How is it with you and God? I'm not suggesting you do something "religious" to "get right with God." But I am asking you to pause a moment and reflect about your relationship with God. Talk with him honestly. Have any barriers been erected between you and God? If so, acknowledge them and ask God to help you remove the blockage.

Humbling ourselves is a big step, one that many of us tremble to take. But it becomes easier to contemplate the more we learn about what God is like. That is where we will turn our attention next.

8

Overcoming the Barriers

WHEN SALLY AND I WERE LIVING IN Afghanistan, we became friends with Ishmael, a good man, a loving and caring man. He was of the Muslim faith, the predominant religion in that country.

In Afghan culture, if you ask a man how many children he has, he will count only the boys. According to their way of thinking, only the boys count because only the boys make money. Girls are a burden. So if a man had four sons and three daughters, and you asked him, "How many children do you have?" he would say, "Four." It was considered a great shame to have no sons at all. In order to maximize his chances of having sons, a man was allowed to take as many as four wives if he wished.

Our friend Ishmael had only one wife, and he had three children, all of them boys. When we met him, his wife was pregnant with her fourth child. We saw Ishmael almost every day, and he was very excited about the new baby to be born. Finally the baby was delivered: another strong, healthy little boy.

When we saw Ishmael a few days later, Sally asked him,

"How is your new baby boy? What name did you give him?"

To our shock and amazement, he replied, "I don't have the little boy anymore."

"*Don't have him anymore*? What happened?" I asked. I was afraid the baby had died.

Ishmael said, "I gave the baby to my neighbor."

Now we were really confused. "You gave him to your neighbor? What do you mean?"

"He had no sons," Ishmael replied simply. "I had four sons. So I gave him one of my sons." Sometimes I try to imagine the look on that neighbor's face when Ishmael walked into his house and presented him with a baby boy.

What was the motive for Ishmael's dramatic gift? He was trying to lift the burden of guilt and shame from his friend's shoulders. The poor fellow felt that he was not a real man. He was embarrassed to go into the marketplace, ashamed to show his face in public. Acting out of deep love for his friend, Ishmael said, in effect, "I want to lift this terrible burden from you." And so he gave the man his own son, unconditionally, no strings attached.

It is almost beyond our comprehension that a father would give away his own son. Who could possibly do such a thing? And yet that is precisely what God did for us, and for the very same reason: to deliver us from our shame. "For God so loved the world that he gave his *only* Son, that whoever believes in him should not perish but have eternal life" (Jn 3:16, italics mine).

THE GIFT OF LOVE

God is all-seeing, all-knowing, and all-powerful, the sovereign ruler over all that he has created. But perhaps the most remarkable thing about God is that he is also *personal*.

He has chosen to make himself "knowable" to his creatures.

God could have created the universe, then stepped back into eternal silence and darkness and never communicated with us at all. But God has not done that. Just the opposite: in every way, at every opportunity, he has sought to reveal himself to us, to say, "I am here. I exist. This is what I am like."

Have you ever noticed how quick we are to blame God when things go wrong in our lives? We verbally shake our fists heavenward and complain, "Why are you doing this to me, God?" Even the insurance companies refer to natural disasters and bizarre accidents as "acts of God."

When we have a problem, how often do we feel deep down inside that God is "finally getting back at us," punishing us for our sins? In our minds, we say that God loves us. But in real life, when we get sick, when something happens to our children, when our marriages get rocky, deep suspicions are aroused but seldom admitted: God must be against us.

When our prayers are not answered the way we hoped, we doubt his concern. When we read of hardships and injustices in the world, we question his justice: "How could a good God allow such things to happen?" When we are depressed or discouraged, we doubt his presence: "Where are you now that I really need you?" We so often struggle to believe— really, honestly *believe*—that God is on our side, that he loves us.

From beginning to end, the Scriptures paint a picture of a God who cares. He created a beautiful world, then created men and women to enjoy the lush garden with him, even to rule over it on his behalf. God created us because he wanted to have *friendship* with us. He gave us the capacity to perceive him, to respond to him, to understand him, to feel him, to choose for him.

Even when the human race disobeyed him and rejected his

love, God pursued us. He gave his laws to Moses. He sent the prophets to speak in his name. And when the nation of Israel broke his laws and stoned his prophets, he took the ultimate step: he sent his only begotten Son to us.

Let me ask you a question. What do you think is the one thing God wants from you more than anything else? Consider the possible answers before you read on…. The fear of the Lord? Obedience to his commands? Repentance from your sins? Total dedication of your life? Your prayers? Your time? Your energies expended in his service? Your money?

In one way or another, of course, God asks us for all these things. But what does he want *most*? What is his highest priority? God desires our hearts.

I knew of a woman many years ago who was married to a very harsh and demanding man, not an easy person to live with. It was a difficult relationship. He was discourteous, demanding, and drunk much of the time. He felt it was his marital right to demand that his wife do certain things for him. If she refused, or if she didn't do them as well as he thought she should have, he felt justified in beating her.

To make sure she knew what he wanted, he would make lists for her. Clean the house. Buy these kinds of food. Run these errands. Naturally, the more she did, the less satisfied he was. Every week the list seemed to get longer and longer. Her torture ended only when her husband was killed in an automobile accident.

A few years later, the woman remarried. Her second husband was a wonderful man and their life together was filled with love. As the years went by, she gradually got past the hurt and pain of her tragic first marriage. It seemed like a distant memory.

Then one day as she was cleaning a bookshelf, a piece of paper fell out of one of the books. It was one of those terrible lists that her first husband used to write for her. She sat down and read it through silently, and as she did all the distant pain swept back over her. She remembered how unloving he was, how demanding. She remembered how she had lived in constant fear of his harsh disapproval.

This woman began to reflect on how different her life was now, on how much her husband loved her, how well he cared for her, how tender he was toward her. Then it suddenly dawned on her: she realized that she happily did far more for her second husband than she had ever done for her first! She usually exceeded the lists of her first husband, not because her second husband demanded it from her, but because it was her greatest joy to serve the one she loved so deeply. Love—her love for him, his love for her—was a far more powerful motivator than fear or guilt.

Many of us think of God as being like the first husband. God has not simply handed us a list of duties and obligations and said, "Here. This is what I want from you. And when you're finished, I have another list for you." The things I mentioned before—obedience, dedication, repentance—are good and right, and things that God *does* very much want from us. But he doesn't want us to do them for the wrong reason. He doesn't want us to fall into religious bondage, trying to please him for the wrong reason.

God simply says to us, "I love you. I love you with all the love there is. There is nothing you could do that would make me love you any more than I already do. And in spite of the fact that you have turned from me more times than you could even count, I still want to be your friend. I still want you to enjoy intimacy with me."

What we are talking about is the difference between what I call "because-of" religion and "in-order-to" religion. This is where Christianity differs from all the other world religions. With them, the starting point is always humankind reaching out for God. But with Christianity, the starting point is God reaching out to the human race—not just once, but again and again and again.

And our heavenly Father doesn't extend his arm in a huge, impersonal, corporate hug. The very nature of love is deeply personal. God loves each one of us individually, and he wants us to love him in return. Out of that love flows our desire to please him.

We don't do things "in order to" earn rewards from God. We don't go to church in order to go to heaven. We don't take communion in order to get God's grace. We don't give God money in order to buy his favor. Whatever we do, we do it "because of" God's love for us, and our love for him.

When we first moved to Holland in 1973, we were introduced to a charming Dutch custom. Whenever you go to someone else's home, it is customary to bring them flowers. In fact, in Holland people seem to give each other flowers all the time—for no reason other than to express friendship. My wife loves this custom, especially when I practice it with her! I like it, too, of course; I enjoy bringing her flowers.

Now imagine that I come home with a bouquet of flowers one afternoon. Sally responds by saying, "Oh, look! Flowers! How lovely! Just wait here while I go get my purse." She runs into the other room and returns in a few seconds with a ten dollar bill. "Here you are," she says.

"What's this for?" I ask in bewilderment.

"It's for the flowers. Ten dollars. I want to pay you for them."

How do you think I would feel in the face of such a response? My heart would sink. I don't buy Sally flowers because I want her to pay me back. I buy her flowers because I love her, and I want to express that love to her in some tangible way.

How often do we treat God the same way? He gives us the gift of life, of love, of forgiveness, of friendship, not because he wants us to say, "Oh! Here, let me pay you back. I'll go to church this Sunday. I'll go out and do some evangelism, maybe feed the poor today." No. God gives us his gifts because he loves us. He wants to be friends with us. And he wants our activities on his behalf to be gifts as well, motivated by our love for him.

God is not a God of religion. He is a God of relationship. He is not out to get us to perform good works for him. He is after our hearts. But God will not demand them or take them by force. He will not seek to win us over through bribery. He will not threaten, or condemn, or manipulate us through guilt or fear. God loves us and relentlessly pursues us with his love. He reveals his heart to us so that we will be drawn to choose a love relationship with him.

HOW DO WE ENTER INTO FRIENDSHIP WITH GOD?

The Bible often uses some new and challenging concepts to describe what God does for us to bring us into relationship with himself (justification, righteousness, regeneration, redemption, etc.). It might be helpful to briefly define a few of those terms so we can appreciate more what has been done for us to overcome the barriers to intimacy with God. It is in reality impossible to separate one aspect of salvation from all the other aspects of what God has done to bring us into friendship with himself. They all intertwine in one grand and glorious blessing of grace.

Justification by Faith. The tragic fact is that each one of us has betrayed God. We have actually rejected the gift of friendship that he has so freely offered. Adam and Eve, by their conscious, deliberate decision to disobey God forfeited the intimate relationship they had once enjoyed with their Creator.

You and I have also made that same conscious, deliberate decision—more times than we could ever count. We have turned away from God. We have disobeyed his laws.

And just as with Adam and Eve, God pronounces a strict punishment for those who break his laws. The Bible says, "... the soul that sins shall die" (Ez 18:4). In another verse we read that "the wages of sin is death" (Rom 6:23). The recompense our disobedience earns for us is eternal separation from God—the demand of his unbreakable justice.

We have sinned: the consequence is death. And yet...

And yet instead of punishing us, God pardons us! Why? Because he loves us. That's it. There is no other reason. It's not because we *deserve* another chance, because we don't. It's not because we're so cute, or so adorable, or so sweet and innocent—because (sorry to have to be so brutally honest) we're not. God pardons us simply and solely because he loves us, and that is what his love prompts him to do.

We can see two important aspects to the pardon God offers. First, it forgives us of past sin; it wipes the slate clean, so to speak. Second, our pardon restores us to full acceptance and friendship with God.

In short, God's pardon establishes a legal peace between him and us. We, by our disobedience, have declared war; but God, out of his great love, declares peace. The only conditions for receiving this pardon—with all the glorious benefits that come with it—are that we sorrowfully *acknowledge* our rebellion against God and gratefully *accept* the indescribable gift he offers. The Bible calls this repentance. This act of heartfelt acknowledgment and acceptance brings pardon and a restored relationship.

A pardoned criminal may be pardoned and set free, but that does not necessarily mean he or she is reconciled to society. Whereas we were once alienated from God because of our sins, God restores us to friendship with himself when he justifies us.

Those who are justified are free from the condemnation of sin, are fully accepted by God, are made heirs to eternal life, are enabled to live a righteous life, and have assurance of being saved from the punishment of their sins (see Rom 8:1; Ti 3:7; Phil 1:11; Rom 5:9).

Regeneration by the Spirit. If justification by faith means we are pardoned and restored to right relationship to God, regeneration has to do with what God does in us. Regeneration means we are given a new heart. It is the new birth (Jn 3:3; Ez 36:26). The result of regeneration is that we become a new creation in Christ Jesus (2 Cor 5:17).

By regeneration a person becomes a child of God and is adopted into the family of God. We become heirs of God and joint heirs with Jesus Christ. We are promised certain privileges, such as knowledge of God's will and provision of our daily needs. The Holy Spirit comes to dwell in our hearts as a result of regeneration, enabling us to overcome temptation (Mt 7:11; 1 Cor 2:10-12; Rom 8:16-17; Eph 1:13-14; 1 Jn 3:9).

Adoption as Sons and Daughters. The legal situation of a son in early Roman times was hardly better than that of a slave. The son was the property of the father, who was legally entitled to the son's earnings. The father could transfer ownership of the son at will, and under certain circumstances, even put him to death.

In contrast, the legally defined status of an adopted son actually put him on a more secure basis than that of a son born into the family. He was no longer liable for old debts, and if he was a slave, he was set free when he was adopted. He had complete and free access to the father of the family. He was guaranteed a position in the family by the adoption.

We become the children of God through our rebirth in Christ. Through adoption we are guaranteed all the rights and privileges associated with the family of God (Jn 1:12-13; Gal 4:6). Paul talks about our adoption in the letter to the Romans: "For you did not receive the spirit of slavery to fall back into fear, but you have received a spirit of sonship. When we cry, 'Abba! Father!' it is the Spirit himself bearing witness with our spirit that we are children of God, and if children, then heirs, heirs of God and fellow heirs with Christ…" (Rom 8:15-16).

In regeneration, we receive a new heart; in justification, a new relationship with God; and in adoption, a new status as sons and daughters of God.

Reconciliation to God. The Bible tells us very bluntly that as sinners we were enemies of God (Rom 5:10). We needed to be reconciled to our Creator. Normally, reconciliation implies that two parties are alienated from one another. But in our relationship to God, he is the innocent party. He has done no wrong. He does not need to be reconciled to us. The Bible nowhere speaks of Christ reconciling God to us.

An enemy is not someone who comes a little short of being a good friend. We should not minimize the seriousness of our former enmity with God. An enemy is in the opposing camp. Sin is rebellion against God, a serious and willful resistance of his love and laws. But Jesus has reconciled us to the Father. "For if while we were enemies we were reconciled to God through the death of his Son,… in Christ God was reconciling the world to himself, not counting our trespasses against us…" (Rom 5:10; 2 Cor 5:19).

Because of Christ's death on the cross, we have been changed from enemies of God to friends! Not only are we forgiven our past sins against him, we are given a new heart to love him. This new spirit within us creates a longing to have fellowship with the very one we once opposed.

Redemption by the Blood of Christ. In the days of slavery, a redeemed person was one who had been set free when the required price had been paid by another. God did not actually pay a price to someone, but rather offered his Son as a ransom, a costly sacrifice, for our sins.

We ourselves were actually *slaves to sin*, but Christ died to set us free. We have "redemption through his blood" (Eph 1:7). Peter wrote that it was "not with perishable things... but with the precious blood of Christ that you were redeemed" (1 Pt 1:18-19).

Each of us becomes a slave through sin: in bondage to guilt, shame, and fear. But when we accept by faith the redemption God offers in Christ, we are set free. We are liberated by the costly death of our dear Lord Jesus—free to be the friends of God.

Repentance from Sin. Repentance refers to a change of mind, actually a radical transformation of thought and attitude, of outlook and direction. It means that we reach a new understanding about our rebellion against God, and make a decision to turn away from our selfish ways to accept God's gift of forgiveness.

Repentance indicates we understand that our sin has grieved the heart of God. We begin to comprehend the horrible nature of our rebellion against a loving God and are struck with deep remorse for what we have done against him and others.

The necessity of repentance as a condition for salvation is clearly taught throughout the Scriptures. Jesus began his public ministry by proclaiming, "Repent, for the kingdom of heaven is at hand" (Mt 4:17). When he gave the disciples the great commission, Jesus instructed them, "... repentance and forgiveness of sins should be preached... to all nations..." (Lk 24:47).

Of course we can in no way earn our salvation through repentance. Salvation is by faith in Christ. We are justified by faith, but we will not be able to receive what we believe if we do not turn from our sins. Repentance is the fruit of a sincere heart, a heart ready to trust in God.

Sanctification by God's Spirit. Sanctification is the process of being made holy. It literally means to be separate. A "holy person" is one who is set apart for God, separated from sin. It does not mean that God does something to us apart from our own surrender, but that we become like Christ as we yield to his will in every area of life.

We become holy by faith and obedience to Christ (Acts 26:18). Luke says that the Holy Spirit is given to those who obey God (Acts 5:32). Holiness is not given to us aside from our own choices to obey God and appropriate the grace of God by faith. We become holy as we obey God and receive his grace to live a godly life.

In another sense, the Bible refers to all Christians as saints or holy ones, because we have been justified by faith and redeemed by the blood of the Lamb. God's Spirit has come to dwell in us; we are new creatures in Christ. We are set apart for God: we are saints! (See Romans 1:7; Ephesians 1:1; Colossians 1:1.)

Sanctification is a *lifelong process*—a process of growth, of learning about God's character, and of applying what we have learned to those areas of our character that need to be changed. We willingly submit to this process not because it *feels* so great, but because we love God and because he dwells within us.

Justification is not a process, but a once-for-all act of God's pardon and restoration to friendship, to right relationship with God. After we have been justified, we enter into the process of sanctification, of being conformed to the nature and character of Christ. We are enabled to do this by the power of Jesus who dwells within us. We choose to obey God, but it is the indwelling Christ that enables us to make the right choices.

Paul summarizes all that God has done for us by telling the believers in Rome that God's children are *made righteous* by faith in Jesus Christ. Paul says this is not a result of obeying religious regulations, but *by faith*. He says in Romans 4:7-8: "Blessed are those whose iniquities are forgiven, and whose sin is covered; blessed is the man against whom the Lord will not reckon his sin."

There it is: we are pardoned, restored, redeemed, adopted, regenerated, reconciled, and made holy! This simple summary in Romans 4:7-8 says it all: "Blessed..." We are blessed! The barrier has been overcome. We are made right with God. Our iniquities are forgiven, our sins are covered, and our punishment is cancelled.

We are right with God!

PERSON TO PERSON

However, for some these theological terms can still seem very abstract. Let's try to make coming into friendship with God more concrete, more personal. Overcoming the barriers to intimacy with our heavenly Father always happens one person at a time.

Sometimes I try to imagine a situation in which I am trying desperately to resolve some conflict or restore a damaged relationship with someone.

I send them letters, but they come back unopened. I try to

phone them, but they won't return my calls.

Finally, since they seem unwilling to deal with me directly, I send my son to speak to them, to explain my desire for reconciliation. And what do they do? They kill him—in fact, they torture him to death. I wonder: what would I do in a situation like that?

The fact is, I'm not sure what I would do. I have a son who is eighteen years old. My son is so very dear to me, I cannot imagine living through such excruciating torment. But I can tell you what *God* did. He said, "I will use your very act of rejection as the instrument of our reconciliation. You used the cross as an implement of torture, but I will use it as the instrument of forgiveness." God took our act of hatred and rebellion and turned it into the source of our restoration. Because of his overwhelming love for us, he found a way to bring us back.

Another story may help us to catch a glimmer of this God who goes out of his way to make a place for us. There was a woman whose son had been killed in World War II. She herself was a devout Christian, but her son had long since turned his back on the church. When the army shipped his body home, she went to the priest and asked that her son be buried in the church cemetery.

This put the priest in a dilemma. He knew how much it meant to the woman to have her son buried in the cemetery, but the law of the church said that only members in good standing could be buried there. Finally, with great sorrow, he had to tell her, "I'm sorry. I can't do it. As much as I would like to, I just can't."

The mother went away broken-hearted.

The priest agonized over the disappointment he had caused this good woman. He tossed and turned all night, thinking about it. Early the next morning he called her. "I want you to have your son's body brought over here," he said. "I want you to have him buried just outside the wall of the cemetery."

"But I don't want him buried outside the cemetery," she said. "I want him buried *inside*."

The priest simply said, "Trust me."

So the woman had her son buried just outside the wall of the cemetery, as the priest had instructed her. The next day she came back to tend the grave, and found to her amazement that the wall had been rebuilt to go around the burial site. The law of the church said he could not be buried inside the cemetery. But no law prohibited the cemetery wall from being moved. Because of his love, the priest had found a way.

God is like that with us. No matter how shabbily we treat him, now matter how resolutely we turn our backs on him, no matter how defiantly we reject him, no matter how big the wall between us, he has found a way to forgive us and welcome us back.

During the Korean war, a pastor in a small rural village awoke one morning to find that his young son, his only child, had been killed. Apparently some soldiers had slipped in during the night and randomly executed a number of villagers in a brutal act of terrorism.

The pastor was beside himself with grief. He had looked forward to his son someday following in his footsteps and becoming a pastor. Now his friends feared for his emotional stability, so severe was the grief he experienced over the boy's senseless death. It seemed so cruel, so unjust. His son was not in the army; he posed no threat to anyone. Why should he have been singled out like this?

Finally the Korean pastor decided what he must do in return for this act of violence. He announced that he would hunt down the men who had killed his son and would not give up until he had found them. No obstacle would stand in his way, no hardship would deter him. This grief-stricken father resolved to do whatever it took.

Amazingly, he was able to learn the identities of the two terrorists, slip behind enemy lines, and find out where they lived. Early one morning he stole into their house and confronted them. The pastor told them who he was, and that he knew they had murdered his son. "You owe me a debt," he said to them. "I have come to collect it."

The two men were obviously expecting to be killed in retaliation. But the pastor's next words astonished them. "You have taken my son," he said, "and now I want you to become my sons in his place."

The pastor stayed with them for several days, until he was able to persuade them to come with him. In time he adopted them as his legal sons. He loved them and cared for them. They became Christians, went to seminary, and were ordained. Today, those two men are pastors in Korea—all because of a father who was willing to do whatever it took to win them, whose love was utterly unstoppable.

That Korean pastor was acting with the very heart of God when he went off in search of those two men, when he poured out his life for them. In his letter to the Ephesians, Paul speaks of "the immeasurable riches of God's grace toward us in Christ Jesus" (see Eph. 2:7). I love that word, "immeasurable." It means that God is always willing to do whatever it takes to show us his mercy and love.

JOHNNY'S SURPRISE

Let me tell you another true story. I know a man who taught at a small college. This professor lived not far from campus and often walked to and from work. He also maintained a fairly regular schedule, so he left in the morning and came back in the afternoon at pretty much the same time each day.

A number of young boys who also lived in the same neighborhood liked to play baseball in their front yards. One day the inevitable happened. One of the boys—we'll call him Johnny—hit a baseball right through the picture window of the professor's house. CRASH!!!

Johnny was terrified. He had never met the professor. He knew him only as a big, serious-looking man who always carried a briefcase and who always came home at three thirty every weekday.

When Johnny looked at his wristwatch and saw that it was three twenty-five, he ran for home as fast as he could. The young boy burst through the front door, charged down the hallway, and dove under his bed. He knew that any minute now, the knock would come at the front door. Obviously the professor would see what had happened and, being so smart, would instantly figure out who was responsible for it. Would he come by himself? Johnny couldn't help but wonder. Or would he call the police? Boy, were his parents going to be mad.

Johnny waited. And waited. And waited. Slowly the realization dawned on him that there would be no knock at the door after all. Maybe the professor *didn't* know who was responsible.

The next day when Johnny went out to play, he noticed that the picture window was no longer broken. It was fixed! Good as new! Just as if nothing had ever happened! Johnny was amazed at his good fortune. He was free! He threw himself into that afternoon's ballgame with greater abandon than ever. Before he knew it, three thirty had rolled around and the professor was making his way up the street.

That same feeling of panic that had overwhelmed him the day before suddenly washed over Johnny a second time. Again he tore off running for home, through the front door, down the hallway, and under the bed.

Now I've really done it, Johnny thought. *How stupid! He's going to know for sure that it was me.* Again the young boy waited for the knock at the door, for the professor to tell his father what he had done. Once again, no knock came. Four o'clock. Four fifteen. Four thirty. Nothing.

Johnny cautiously opened the door and peeked outside. No professor. No police.

But Johnny couldn't shake the feelings of fear and guilt. Do you know what little boys' faces look like when they know they're guilty of some serious misdeed and are just waiting for someone to call out their name in anger? That's what Johnny's face looked like all through dinner—and for the next several days. His life felt like a nightmare. Every afternoon, when he saw the professor come around the corner, he took off running.

One day, however, when Johnny saw the professor and started to run, the professor dropped his briefcase and started chasing after him! Johnny kept running, but it was no use. The professor caught him by the arm, whirled him around, and held him tightly so he couldn't get away. He got on his knees, looked Johnny right in the eye, and said, "I know it was you, Johnny. I know you're the one who broke my window."

Johnny felt as though he were about to faint.

"But Johnny," the man said, "I forgive you. I've already paid for the window. I know how these things happen. I've done it myself. Johnny, I don't want you to be afraid of me. I don't want you to run from me. I want you to be my friend. Will you be my friend, Johnny?"

Johnny looked up into the professor's face. Do you know what he said? The boy yelled, "I hate you!" And he ran away as fast as his short legs could carry him.

The next day, the professor did the same thing—except this time he came home ten minutes early. He caught Johnny again, knelt down to look him in the eye, and said, "Johnny, listen to me! I've paid for it. Do you understand? I've paid for it. I forgive you. It's okay."

Johnny just stood there, trembling with fear. The professor said, "Johnny, all I want is for us to be friends. I can't stand it that we can't be friends." And the grown man started to cry. Finally Johnny couldn't take it any more, and he started to cry, too. "Thank you," the boy sobbed. "Thank you for being my friend."

Much the same poignant drama unfolds between God and us. We *know*, deep in our hearts, that we have hurt and offended God, and in our shame and guilt we hide from him. Even when we hear how merciful and forgiving he is, we don't know how to respond. Sometimes in our fear, we reject him yet again. But God pursues us still. And in the end, if we will let him, the Father will take us in his arms, and tell us that he forgives us, and that he loves us.

God wants to be our friend. And he is willing to do whatever it takes.

9

You Are My Friends If You Obey Me

W HAT ARE SOME OF THE QUALITIES that go into a good
friendship?

When I think of a good friend, I think of someone with
whom I share common interests. Someone I like to spend
time doing things with. Someone who accepts me as I am,
who encourages me. Someone I can tell secrets to without fear
of betrayal. Someone who will tell me the truth when I need
to hear it. Someone I can count on. Someone I must obey.

Hold on just a minute, you say. *"Someone I must obey?"*
That sounds like a parent, or a boss, or a commanding officer... but not a friend. What does obedience have to do with
friendship?

Plenty, according to Jesus. Listen to what he has to say on
the subject:

"As the Father has loved me, so have I loved you; abide in
my love. If you keep my commandments, you will abide in

my love, just as I have kept my Father's commandments
and abide in his love. These things I have spoken to you,
that my joy may be in you, and that your joy may be full.

"This is my commandment, that you love one another as
I have loved you. Greater love has no man than this, that a
man lay down his life for his friends. *You are my friends if
you do what I command you.*"   Jn 15:9-14, emphasis mine

There you have it in plain black and white: our obedience
is a condition of intimacy with God. It is not a condition of
salvation, but of growing friendship and intimacy with the
Lord Jesus. We are his friends *if* we do what he commands us.
We might expand the thought to say we will be friends of
Jesus *to the extent that* we do what he commands us. Greater
obedience brings greater intimacy. Disobedience is an inevitable barrier to growth in our friendship with God.

A MEAN OLD MAN WHO CARRIES A BIG STICK?

Why would Jesus say something like this? Actually, he
makes his motivation clear in the passage itself. He says, "I
have told you this so that my joy may be in you, and so that
your joy may be complete." So we remind ourselves again:
this is not teaching about salvation by works. We discussed
what God has done for us in the last chapter to overcome
every barrier to friendship with God. This passage teaches us
how to grow in that friendship. We do not usually think of
obedience as being linked with joy. To most of us, obedience
is usually connected more with thoughts of dry duty. But
Jesus speaks of a direct connection: more obedience, more
joy; less obedience, less joy. Now we could take this admonition and run with it in a number of different directions. Many
of us pull out the church rule book—whether literal or figura-

tive. But God is not looking for mechanical obedience to arbitrary rules. Our heavenly Father is not some sour-faced, mean-spirited, black-robed, stick-carrying old man sitting up there making up rules to make us miserable. He is not like one of those stereotypical sheriffs in the American deep South who set ridiculously low speed limits, and then hide behind billboards waiting gleefully to arrest people when they cruise by too fast.

God loves us. All of his actions toward us are designed to bring us further into relationship with himself, to make it easier for us to share intimacy. One of the things God does to foster relationship is to show us what he himself is like. And one of the ways he shows us what he is like is by giving us his moral laws. God's commands—his laws, his standards, his precepts, call them what you will—are reflections of his character.

When God gives us his laws, he is saying to us, "This is what I am like. If you will live in accordance with what I am like, you will experience joy and peace and fulfillment in life. I am loving, so love one another. I create life, so do not kill one another. I give, so don't steal. I've created you to be like me, to share my image and likeness. If you live the way I've created you to live, you'll be happy. If you don't, you'll be unhappy."

That makes sense, doesn't it? Think for a moment about Ford Motor Company. They spend a lot of time and energy and money designing automobiles. They have a pretty clear idea of what their automobiles were and were not designed to do. They also have a lot of wisdom about how their automobiles are best cared for. If consumers use their automobiles according to what they were designed for, and care for them according to the manufacturer's instructions, each car will serve the owner well. If not... the driver can certainly expect trouble, sooner or later.

For example, automobiles are meant to be driven on roads, and they are meant to be powered by gasoline. Now suppose you say to yourself, "Well, I really don't like gasoline all that much. It's expensive and it smells bad. I'm just not a gasoline kind of guy. I'm more of a diet cola type. And driving on roads all the time gets awfully monotonous. Why shouldn't I be able to take a more scenic route and cruise down the river for a change?" That adventurous driver sure wouldn't get very far.

I remember walking out of my apartment in Amsterdam one morning and seeing a man who had apparently been thinking along these lines. (Actually, I think he had been doing more drinking than thinking.) He meandered over to his car—one of the old Volkswagen "Bugs"—climbed in, started the engine, put it in gear, and drove straight into one of the many canals that wind their way through the city.

Now one of the interesting things about the old VW's was that they were nearly air-tight, and could actually float in water for a quite a while. So this fellow merrily made his way down the canal, pushing down on the gas pedal and turning the steering wheel, just as if he were really driving on water.

Sooner or later, though, you can bet he discovered his mistake. No matter how much we might like it to be so, cars just aren't designed to work that way. He would have learned a similar lesson if he had tried to fill his fuel tank with diet cola.

Human life is much the same. If we expect it to work smoothly, we've got to function in accordance with the manufacturer's instructions. In our case, the "owner's manual" is the Bible, divinely inspired yet written by human hands. God says, "This is what I am like—and what you are like as well. These laws are a reflection of who I am. If you follow them, you'll experience joy in intimacy with me. If you go against them, you'll be going against my nature, and against your own nature as well. What's more, I have set into being a cause-and-effect system of consequences. If you disregard or disobey my laws, you'll inherit the consequences."

This is where we so often get the wrong idea. We often imagine a mean-spirited God punishing us for infractions of the rules. In fact, what we have is a merciful God who allows us to experience the consequences of our mistakes—precisely so we'll learn not to do them again!

When we look at it that way, we begin to see how pointless it is to blame God for the negative consequences of our actions, as though he were simply "out to get us" like the sheriff behind the billboard. We really have no one to blame but ourselves. Repentance offers us the way back to joy. The more quickly we acknowledge our mistake and change our ways, the sooner we'll be back on the road to enjoying intimacy with God.

RELIGION WITHOUT RELATIONSHIP

Of course, all this has to do with things more serious than automobiles. I think of a friend of mine, a Bible teacher, who was invited to speak on sexual morality at a secular college. The other speakers were proponents of the familiar free-love, free-sex philosophy. My friend suspected he'd been called in just so they could make a spectacle of him.

When it came his turn to speak, he said simply, "I really love sex. I think it is great. I enjoy it regularly." My friend went on to speak of how his marriage commitment created the boundaries of security and trust that made possible the sexual fulfillment God intended between man and woman.

Now on most college campuses, the Christian teaching on sex is not terribly popular. Many students think of it as "a bunch of restrictive rules designed to deny me the happiness I'm entitled to." But when my friend finished speaking, the audience gave him a standing ovation. Those students were able to understand that day that in sex, as in so many other areas, it just makes sense to follow the manufacturer's instructions.

Is it becoming a bit clearer now why Jesus talks about friendship and obedience in the same breath? His motivation in giving us his law is so that our friendship can thrive. At the same time, *our* motivation for obedience will ideally flow from friendship, too. Jesus is saying, "I hope our friendship will mean enough to you that you'll *want* to obey, not just feel that you *have* to obey." Such a response reflects the difference between an *internalized* relationship and an *imposed* relationship.

One of the saddest things in Christianity today is the number of people who have *religion* but not *relationship*. For them, Christianity isn't a matter of "want-to" but of "have-to." They more often feel obligation rather than exhilaration in serving the Lord. "What will people think of me if I don't come to the midweek prayer meeting? What will happen to me if I don't come to the worship service on Sunday? Don't sing in the choir? Don't put money in the collection plate?"

These folks are missing the whole point—and all the joy! Let me give another example. In Holland, where I lived for many years, people tend to be fairly tolerant. Dutch laws are not too numerous or overly restrictive. They do, however, have a law against wife-beating. Now it just so happens that I didn't violate that law while I lived in Holland (or anywhere else, for that matter). I have never beaten my wife, not once. Why? Because there's a law against it? Because I'm afraid of getting into trouble with the Anti-Wife-Beating Police?

No! The reason I treat my wife right isn't because there's a law against it. I treat her right because I love her! Because I have a relationship with her. I have a heart-driven desire to care for her. Because of that, I actually go far beyond what the law requires. Not only do I not beat her but I also treat her tenderly and respectfully.

That's how it's supposed to work between us and the Lord. If we find ourselves going through life always looking over our shoulders, asking, "Can I get away with this? Is this okay according to the law?" then we're missing the point. People who are in love don't ask what is the *least* they're required to do for one another. They just naturally gravitate toward doing the most they can.

Motivation makes all the difference in the world—the difference between fear and love, between obligation and relationship, between guilt and grace, between friendship and performance.

You might expect that a chapter on the importance of obedience would focus on rules. You might be looking for a long list of rules and regulations, do's and don'ts, with an explanation of how following them will win you greater intimacy with God.

Well, if that's what you're expecting, I'm afraid I'm going to disappoint you. I hope I've shown you by now that laying down "hard-and-fast rules for a good friendship" is not what the Bible teaches. That idea contributes to "religiosity," to a system of trying to earn God's approval through our performance. That is always a dead end.

At the same time, I'm certainly not proposing that the Bible contains no commandments, no standards. One approach to Christianity does take such a position. It's called *antinomianism*, from the Latin for "opposed to all rules," and it is a heresy. God does not operate on the basis that "anything goes." As we have seen, he shows us what he himself is like, then calls us to act in accordance with his nature. If we do so, we experience what Jesus called "fullness of joy." If we don't, we experience the negative consequences.

What is important, then, is not to memorize a bunch of

petty rules, but to get as clear an idea as possible of what God is like, so that we can act in accordance with his nature. As we have said in other contexts, we could easily spend the rest of our lives plumbing the depths of the character and nature of God. All we can do in a short chapter like this is to make a humble beginning.

OBEDIENCE FROM THE HEART

Having said all that, I would like to consider a few aspects of God's character in terms of how it would affect our lives if we obey God from the heart. To the degree that we come to know God, to the degree that we desire intimacy with him, we will naturally want our thoughts and words and actions to correspond to these qualities.

The faithfulness of God inspires us to be faithful in return. Faithfulness can be a rather nebulous concept. Faithfulness to whom? To what? To God? To our friends? To our promises? Our marriages? Our families? Obviously the answer is yes to all of these. But faithfulness on that kind of grand scale can be difficult for us to work with in a day-to-day way.

Knowing the weakness of our human frame, Jesus helps bring it down to a level where we can more easily grab hold: "He who is faithful in a very little is faithful also in much; and he who is dishonest in a very little is dishonest also in much. If then you have not been faithful in the unrighteous mammon [money and the goods of this world], who will entrust to you the true riches? And if you have not been faithful in that which is another's, who will give you that which is your own?" (Lk 16:10-12).

The principle is simple: faithfulness in great things is foreshadowed by faithfulness in small things, and faithfulness in spiritual matters is foreshadowed by faithfulness in natural affairs. We could also turn it around to say this: the way to grow in faithfulness concerning grand, spiritual matters is to practice faithfulness in small, earthly matters.

Love motivates us to faithfulness. When our love for God and our love for others is strong, faithfulness will be part of the overflow of our hearts. Perhaps one of the reasons we don't grow in our spiritual lives, one of the reasons our intimacy with God languishes, is because God gave us something small and seemingly insignificant to do and we disdained it as unimportant. But often it is the seemingly unimportant matters that are the most important of all to God.

I remember one of the first missionary trips I helped lead, more than twenty-five years ago. We were taking about two hundred fifty young people to Jamaica for the summer, and I was excited to be part of it. I went to the man who was in charge and said, "What can I do to help?"

"Well," he said, "I'll tell you what I really need. Down in the basement we have a bunch of literature that was shipped down here, and we need to get it organized. Could you handle that for me?"

"Sure," I said, delighted to be of help. "No problem."

Then I went downstairs, where I discovered boxes and boxes and boxes of printed materials—all of them water-stained. I don't know how it happened. Maybe they got left out in the rain. Or maybe they fell off the boat while they were being unloaded. In any case, they were a mess.

"Oh, man," I inwardly groaned. "This is going to take twenty years!" It didn't take twenty years, of course. But it did take days. I had to unpack the boxes, lay out the materials so they could dry, then get everything sorted and bundled and boxed and tied together.

I don't mind telling you, I went through some interesting

spiritual exercises in my mind while doing all this work. "This is ridiculous," I thought. "I didn't come here for this. I came to hand out tracts, not stack them. I came to serve the Lord!"

Little did I realize that my mundane assignment was a crash course in God's school of faithfulness. Was my love for him great enough to overflow into faithfulness in this seemingly insignificant chore?

Any of us who have ever tried to run a business or manage a department or chair a committee know how hard it is to find people who will be faithful in the little things. God is looking for the same kind of people, men and women who will be faithful from the heart simply because they want to please him.

We are called to extend God's forgiveness to others. We know that God has forgiven us. And the Bible tells us over and over again that we must forgive others. Jesus goes so far as to tell us that we must forgive our enemies, and pray for those who "despitefully use us" (see Lk 6).

Have you ever been hurt by someone? Ever been used? Betrayed? Has anyone ever done anything to you that seemed like sheer manipulation? Given you the short end of the stick in a round of office—or church—politics? What do you do with those hurt feelings?

What does Jesus say to do? He says, "Forgive."

It does no good to pull an abscessed tooth if you end up leaving the painful roots behind. In the same way, before we can forgive, we have to get to the root of the pain. Not just the facts of what happened, but the roots of how it affected us inside. We need to take time to analyze why it hurt so much. "It hurts because he said one thing and then did something else." "It hurts because now I feel like I can't trust him." "It hurts because in retrospect I can see the way he set me up."

Whatever the problem is, we need to call it what it is. Far

too many Christians remain mired in what the psychologists call "denial." They've never let themselves face what's really troubling them. They try to put a positive "spin" on everything, try to pretend that the negative experiences never really happened.

Such an approach leads to what I call the "trash compactor" syndrome. Do you know what a trash compactor is? It's a device that takes all our garbage and crams it together into a tight little package. A lot of people do that with their feelings: they pack them down inside, trying to pretend they aren't there. But of course they *are* there. And sooner or later this emotional garbage will need to be properly disposed of.

As a young adult, I rarely talked about my feelings. If I was angry, I didn't let on. I tried to pretend everything was "fine." Or if I was impatient, or frustrated, or frightened, I just crammed it down inside and went on as if it never happened—the trash compactor syndrome.

I remember the first time someone said to me, "Floyd, you never deal with your feelings." I couldn't figure out what on earth he was talking about. "You're not in touch with your emotions," he said. "You don't know what they are. You don't even have names for them."

Eventually I discovered an important truth: God created us as emotional beings. Our feelings—even the negative, unpleasant ones—are not a result of the fall. They were built into us by God from the beginning. They are like the warning lights on the dashboard of a car. Automobiles are designed in such a way that there's a direct relationship between those bright red lights and what's going on inside the engine.

In the same way, there is a connection between what we're feeling and what's going on inside of us. It is vital, for our own health as well as for our relationships with others, that we learn to identify our feelings, to describe them, to communicate them—to take them seriously.

It is also vital that we recognize that forgiveness is a process. We often wish it weren't the case, but there is no getting around it. Imagine that you've just had an accident of some sort. Your arm has been lacerated and the bone broken. You go to the doctor, and he says, "Well, today let's clean out the wound and set the bone, then tomorrow…"

You break in, "But wait a minute. I don't want to come back tomorrow. I want you to heal it *now*." Can you see that repairing the damage to your arm wouldn't work that way? In the same way, healing is a process. The deeper the wound, the longer the restoration may require.

It is the same with forgiveness. We would like for it to be a quick, clean, once-and-for-all action: someone hurts us, we forgive them, that's that. Simple and relatively painless micro-surgery. But in real life, it doesn't work that way. Forgiveness is a process. Someone hurts us. We forgive them. Then to-morrow—or next week, or next month—we see them or think of them, and the pain and anger are still there. So we forgive them again. And again. And again. As often as it takes.

Forgiveness is not a whitewash job, not a cover-up, not pretending that what happened wasn't wrong, or didn't hurt, or never happened in the first place. Rather, it is recognizing that what happened *was* wrong, and *did* hurt, and still *does* hurt. It is continuing to forgive, again and again—until we can look at the other person with nothing in our hearts but the love of God for them.

As we make that choice to forgive—over and over again if necessary—God will fill our hearts with his love for the person. Forgiveness is the love of God, deep in our hearts, welling up and overflowing toward those who have caused us pain. It is a process of pardoning someone who has sinned against us.

God's forbearance is another aspect of his character that will affect our obedience. Forbearance means "bearing with one another despite their weaknesses and failings." It is in this category that the scriptural commands about "not judging" come into play. All of us know there is nothing that makes us feel more unloved than to be judged by other people. And all of us know that Jesus was quite clear on the subject: "Judge not, that you be not judged" (Mt 7:1).

One of the problems many of us have is that we have never learned the difference between *judgment* and *discernment,* two words which both come from the same Greek root. To discern means to see what is there, to acknowledge what is good, or bad, or right, or wrong, or whatever the case may be. To judge is to go one step further: it is to condemn, to pass sentence, to write someone off, to cut them off from yourself or, at least in your own estimation, to cut them off from God's favor. To judge a person is to go beyond disagreeing with them; it is to assign sinful or selfish motives to their actions.

When Jesus tells us not to judge others, he's not telling us to "wear blinders," to ignore what we see or to pretend it isn't there. He's not telling us to act as though wrong things were right. That's *discernment.* It is only when we take the next step that we have wrongly judged them: when we put ourselves on the throne and begin passing sentence on others and on their motivation.

Many times we will see things in other people's lives that we disagree with or don't like. Some things merely irritate us; other things we believe—or know—to be wrong. The closer fellowship we enjoy with someone, in fact, the more such weaknesses and failings we will be able to see. This can actually serve as a test of our relationships: if we don't know one another's weaknesses, then we probably don't know one another very well.

Forbearance is getting close enough to others so that we see their weaknesses, but loving them enough that we do not judge them. Rather, we choose to walk alongside of them as they go through the process of dealing with their problems.

Obedience to Jesus includes welcoming the little ones, the weak ones, the ones who are hurting. This fourth aspect of God's character and our obedience is illustrated in the following exchange between Jesus and his disciples: "An argument arose among them as to which of them was the greatest. But when Jesus perceived the thought of their hearts, he took a child and put him by his side, and said to them, "Whoever receives this child in my name receives me" (Lk 9:46-48).

We can know we're on the right track if we have time for "the little people." If we think we're too important for other people, if we make ourselves untouchable and invulnerable to their need and their pain, we have much more to learn about the love of God.

Jesus takes the point even further in the parable of the Good Samaritan. We all know the story: a man is beaten and left by the side of the road for dead. Three "religious" people pass him by. Only one man stops to help him. I think that part of what Jesus is saying through this parable is that if we are his friends, we will be people who touch the shame of others without recoiling in horror.

Touching the shame of others. A powerful concept. Think about the Samaritan. He didn't just drop a few extra coins in the offering plate. He didn't just mail in a check in response to a direct-mail fundraising appeal for the care of injured strangers. He didn't just have his employer deduct a contribution to the United Fund from his paycheck. He bent down and touched the man as he lay mired in his nakedness, his woundedness, his shame. He carried him to the inn on his own donkey and personally cared for the man's injuries. He acted like Jesus would in that situation. He obeyed from the heart, in response to a man in need.

The fifth quality of God's character as it relates to our obedience is accountability. Jesus instructed us to exhort and admonish one another in our selfishness and to call one another on to holiness. No one was more accountable in his actions and attitudes than the Lord Jesus: "I have given them the words which thou gavest me,... while I was with them, I kept them in thy name..." (Jn 17:8, 12). He was under the authority of the Father and open and accountable to the disciples.

He shared his greatest burdens with them in the garden of Gethsemane. He related the temptations he faced in the wilderness. He communicated his disappointments and burdens.

The Bible teaches us to confess our sins and our burdens to one another (Gal 6:1-2; Jas 5:16). And it teaches us to confront one another as well. "If your brother sins against you, go and tell him his fault" (Mt 18:15). I believe this may be the most neglected command in the Bible.

We find confrontation so difficult! When someone sins against us, we'll do almost anything but address it directly. We'll get angry, we'll get hurt, we'll get defensive, we'll get filled with self-pity. We'll even go talk to other people about it. But the last thing we'll usually do is go to the person who wronged us, look him or her in the eye, and say, "We need to talk."

Perhaps the only thing harder than confronting others is *being* confronted. But we need it. Accepting the admonition and exhortation of others is an indispensable ingredient to our obeying God.

I have a friend who works as a management consultant. He begins any professional relationship by asking the top leader, "Who in this organization can say no to you and get away with it?" If the answer is, "nobody," then that becomes the starting point. Accountability is crucial. How about you? Is there anyone in your life who can say no to you and get away with it?

Count Zinzendorf founded the Moravians, a tremendously fruitful Christian renewal movement that began in Germany in 1727. The Count was on the receiving end of a great deal of criticism. The surrounding population was almost entirely Lutheran or Catholic, and individuals from both groups would often write him letters of criticism or condemnation.

Most of us, if we got letters like that, would throw them away before anyone saw them. Zinzendorf used to read his out loud to the congregation! Then he would say, "Please, whatever truth there is in these criticisms, point it out to me so I can correct it." What an example of courage and humility!

When I was in Bible school, one professor believed it was best not to let people get too close to you if you happened to be a minister. I was taught to always have those I lead call me "Reverend McClung." Too much familiarity would cause them to lose respect for me—or so I was told.

In fact, I have found just the opposite to be true. It is precisely when people *can* get close—when they can see our faults, when they feel secure enough to confront us about our faults—that they respect us, if we respond in humility.

I need to make myself accountable to other Christians. You need to make yourself accountable as well. We all need it. We need to invite other people to speak into our lives, and we need to commit ourselves to confronting them when the need arises. We need to be more open with our friends, with our colleagues, with our spouses. It is an indispensable overflow of love in our lives.

Jesus said, "you are my friends if you obey what I command you." Obedience is an overflow of love. I've touched on only a few particular aspects of this truth. Needless to say, I could mention many other ways in which our love is supposed to overflow in obedience to the Lord. But this is a beginning at least. The more we walk in obedience to the Lord's commands, the more we will experience his blessing. And the more prepared we will be to respond to God's "friendly fire."

10

Friendly Fire

THE VIETNAM WAR INTRODUCED a number of new words and phrases into the English language. One of the most fascinating was "friendly fire," a particularly twisted euphemism developed by the Army to describe an especially tragic instance: when its soldiers were killed, not by the enemy, but accidently by their own comrades.

As Christians, we may sometimes get the feeling that *we* are encountering "friendly fire." In fact, some of our most painful trials and difficulties seem to come from sources that we thought were supposed to be on our side. Our fellow believers, for example. Or even God himself.

Have you ever felt as though God were firing on you? You just might have been right!

All the commandments which I command you this day you shall be careful to do, that you may live and multiply, and go in and possess the land which the LORD swore to give to your fathers. And you shall remember all the ways in which the LORD your God has led you these forty years in the wilderness, that he might humble you, testing you to know what was in your heart, whether you would keep his commandments, or not.   Dt 8:1-2

This passage, and many others like it, says what many of us are reluctant to acknowledge: that God tests us. That some of the challenges we face in life are not just the result of our old enemies, the world, the flesh, and the devil. That most of our trials and difficulties come with God's stamp of approval, in order that he might refine—and that we might see for ourselves—our weaknesses as they are revealed under fire.

GOD'S TOUGH LOVE

God is not mean, nor does he take some sort of perverse delight in seeing us squirm. When he tests us, it is most definitely for our good. Ultimately, God's tough love is intended to help us grow closer to him. The writer of the letter to the Hebrews understood this principle:

And have you forgotten the exhortation which addresses you as sons?—"My son, do not regard lightly the discipline of the Lord,/ nor lose courage when you are punished by him./ For the Lord disciplines him whom he loves,/ and chastises every son whom he receives." It is for discipline that you have to endure. God is treating you as sons... he disciplines us for our good, that we may share his holiness. For the moment all discipline seems painful rather than pleasant; later it yields the peaceful fruit of righteousness to those who have been trained by it.   Heb 12:5-7, 10-11

Several points in this passage need to be emphasized. First, notice that the passage is talking about *sons* (and daughters, of course), about God's beloved children. Discipline is part of the package when we become part of God's family. Unlike so many of our earthly friends, the Father does not simply ignore or overlook our sins and character defects. Rather, he takes it upon himself to help correct them.

This passage from Hebrews also makes clear that the motivation behind God's discipline is *always love*. When we experience God's hand of correction or testing, our first inclination is often to ask, "Why is God always picking on me?" In reality, he disciplines us precisely because he loves us.

Third, the passage says that God's aim is to help us share in his *holiness*. God's discipline and testing bears not only a "negative," corrective aspect, but also a positive aspect. Where we are wrong, God will certainly aim to set us right; where we are weak, he will make every effort to strengthen us.

But there is more. Even where we are already strong, God will seek to make us stronger; where we are already holy, he will seek to make us holier still. The ultimate goal was stated by Jesus: "You, therefore, must be perfect, as your heavenly Father is perfect" (Mt 5:48). And when you think about it, why would a God of love settle for anything less?

Fourth, the passage shows that even though discipline is often unpleasant, in time it proves to be worthwhile. Haven't we all seen this principle played out in our lives? I remember when I was a little boy, learning to swim down at the YMCA. The group of college students who instructed us were real sticklers for proper form. They made me keep my head down when I turned it to take a breath. They made me keep my legs straight when I kicked. They never let me cut short the number of lengths in the pool I was supposed to swim.

My feelings toward those swimming instructors were often marked by something less than perfect Christian charity.

Today, however, I appreciate what they did for me. I'm a good swimmer to this day because of the discipline they applied.

Let me ask you a question: Have you ever attended a meeting where someone issued a challenge to be more Christ-like, more yielded to the Holy Spirit, more totally surrendered to the will of God? And did you say yes? Did you tell the Lord you wanted to be more like him, no matter what it took?

Now let me ask you another question: Why do you complain when God tests you or disciplines you? When he arranges situations and circumstances that expose your weaknesses and challenge you to grow, he is simply taking you seriously and answering your prayer! We should be grateful.

Most often, God tests us through other people. "Iron sharpens iron," the Bible says, "and one man sharpens another" (Prv 27:17). When we experience this "sharpening" from a brother or sister in the Lord—sometimes people call it "sandpaper ministry"—it is really the Lord who is at work through them.

But God is also quite capable of acting directly in our lives. One illustration comes from the life of David. When David became king, he united the twelve tribes of Israel for the first time in generations. He had defeated all of Israel's enemies. Now David sought to restore worship to God's temple.

> And they carried the ark of God upon a new cart.... And David and all the house of Israel were making merry before the LORD with all their might.... And when they came to the threshing floor of Nacon, Uzzah put out his hand to the ark of God and took hold of it, for the oxen stumbled. And the anger of the LORD was kindled against Uzzah; and God smote him there because he put forth his hand to the ark; and he died there beside the ark of God. And David was angry because the LORD had broken forth upon Uzzah.... 2 Sm 6:3-8

The sudden death of Uzzah strikes me as a case of "God's friendly fire." David had shown in other instances that he understood the importance of doing God's work in God's way, of waiting on the Lord for instructions. But in this case, he seems to have forgotten that lesson. King David had a program, an agenda. He knew what he wanted to do, and how he wanted to do it, and when he wanted it done by.

The account says that David had the ark carried on a new cart. I've discovered that God is not all that impressed with new carts. He's not particularly impressed by our goals and plans and committees and timetables. God wants us to do his work *his* way.

Being his friends does not mean that we can presume upon God, that we can casually do our own thing and expect him to "bless us regardless." How often do we charge into action, praying that the Lord will bless our efforts? But it's supposed to be the other way around: our actions are supposed to bless *him*. We are, in fact, supposed to do what God has decided to bless. David was trying to do the right thing, but he was doing it the wrong way. God disciplined him severely for it, and Uzzah got caught in the crossfire.

God has a special plan, a special destiny for each one of us. If we do not discern and pass the tests God puts us through, we will not inherit our destiny. I estimate that the vast majority of Christians do not enter into their destiny in God. They do not take seriously God's testings in their life. They give up when the heat gets turned up. They won't take the pressure, so they give up. They quit. They don't backslide, they just settle for second best. What about you? Are you a quitter or are you committed to inherit all God has for you regardless of the cost?

I find it interesting to note that the next time David transports the ark, he doesn't use a new cart! He had learned an important lesson.

Every test sent by God contains three parts:

1. The difficult circumstances that make it a test.
2. The desired reaction God wants from us to the particular challenges we face.
3. The resulting growth that takes place in our lives as we respond rightly to those trying circumstances.

David learned from the testings God put him through. His example points up the great importance of responding properly to God's testing and discipline. A correct response to God's testing always involves these two elements:

- First, the *attitude of our heart* must be such that God's discipline can take root deep within. That means remaining teachable and humble, so we can accept and apply what God is teaching us.
- Second, we must have *trust in God's character*. We need to live with the expectation that the Lord will, from time to time, intervene in our circumstances to test us. This trust will manifest itself in a receptive attitude to the difficult circumstances of our life.

Another classic example of God's dealings with one of his children is the biblical story of Joseph.

FROM BAD TO WORSE

Joseph was the youngest of twelve brothers. The fact that he was his father's favorite did nothing to endear him to his older brothers: "But when his brothers saw that their father loved him more than all his brothers, they hated him, and could not speak peaceably to him" (Gn 37:4). Not exactly a terrific situation. And it grew *worse* as time passed.

When Joseph was just a youth of seventeen, he began having mysterious dreams. In one of these dreams, he and his
brothers were binding sheaves of grain in a field. "And lo,"
Joseph told his brothers, "my sheaf arose and stood upright;
and behold, your sheaves gathered round it, and bowed down
to my sheaf."

His brothers were quick to catch on to what the dream
meant. "Are you indeed to reign over us?" they said. "Are
you indeed to have dominion over us?" The Bible says that
Joseph's brothers "hated him yet more for his dreams and for
his words" (Gn 37:7-8).

But it got even *worse*. Joseph had another dream, which he
again shared with his brothers. "Behold, I have dreamed
another dream," he said; "and behold, the sun, the moon,
and eleven stars were bowing down to me" (Gn 37:9). Even
his father was displeased by the implication that he, too,
would one day be subservient to his own son. Perhaps Joseph
shouldn't have been so forthright!

For his brothers, this was the last straw; they made up their
minds to kill him—all except for his more tender-hearted
brother Reuben, who decided to try to trick his brothers.
"Let's not kill him," Reuben said, "at least not directly. Let's
just toss him into this pit and let starvation and wild animals
do the deed for us. That way it will look like an accident" (see
Gn 37:19-24).

Reuben's plan was to come back later and release Joseph so
that he could escape. But it didn't work out that way. Just
after Joseph's brothers had cast him into the pit, they saw a
caravan of Ishmaelites making its way across the plain. Judah,
one of the older brothers, had an idea.

"What's the point of just leaving him to die?" he said.
"Let's sell him to these traders. Then at least we can make
some money on the deal. And we won't have his blood on
our hands, either." Big-hearted guy, that Judah. And that is

exactly what they did. When Reuben came back later to help Joseph out of the pit, his youngest brother was already gone —sold into slavery (see Gn 37:25-30).

By this time, Joseph was probably not too pleased about what appeared to be God's plan for his life! For a seventeen-year-old boy in those days, things couldn't have gotten much worse. And to think he was in this terrible situation because of the actions of his own brothers! Can you imagine yourself in such painful circumstances?

But the fact was, Joseph *was* right square in the middle of God's plan for his life. In time, through a series of improbable circumstances and even worse troubles, he finally became a great ruler in the land of Egypt. Joseph used his power to save not only his father and brothers but also the entire Jewish people from extinction. And in the end, his father and his brothers actually *did* bow down before him, just as Joseph's dreams had foretold.

Notice especially that the very people who were opposing the dream—who, as far as they knew, were acting to *prevent* its fulfillment—actually became the *instruments* of its fulfillment. I wonder how often you and I miss God's purposes in the circumstances of our lives because we're so angry at the people who oppose us that we don't realize they're the very people God is using to bring us into our destiny! Barriers made by human hands can be God's opportunities to prepare us for what he intends.

Many years later, Joseph's father and brothers stood before him and recognized him for who he was. When he saw their terrible guilt over what they had tried to do to him, Joseph summed up the meaning of the whole story. "As for you," he said to his brothers, "you meant evil against me; but God meant it for good" (Gn 50:20). Joseph was able to see the hand of God in all that had happened to him.

The trick, of course, is to be able to trust that God's hand is in our difficulties while they are still happening, long before we see the final outcome. I believe that God builds into our lives the foundations for the plans he has chosen for us. Before we enter into our destiny, we must go through God's testings, which are designed to season us, to temper us, to bring us to maturity.

A THIEF IS A THIEF

I learned more about responding correctly to God's friendly fire through something that happened to me several years ago. The story concerns a simple incident, but the lesson was a serious and important one.

We were living at the time on a pair of houseboats anchored in the harbor of Amsterdam. There were about sixty of us altogether: our family, eight or nine staff members, and a large number of very challenging young Christians: hippies, dropouts, addicts, prostitutes—a whole range of brand new believers.

We had a common kitchen and dining area. In the kitchen were two refrigerators: one that anyone could raid at any time, and one that held the food for our community meals. No one but the cooks was allowed to take food from the second refrigerator without permission.

One night I couldn't sleep and I felt hungry, so I went down to the kitchen. It was late; everyone on the houseboat was asleep. I looked inside the "open" refrigerator. Nothing. I looked inside the other refrigerator. There it was: a tall glass of cold milk.

I love cold milk, and right at that moment I wanted that glass of milk more than anything. But there was a problem. *No one* was supposed to take anything from that refrigerator without permission.

On the other hand, I thought, maybe that wasn't such a big problem. After all, I told myself, I was the head of the community. I could give myself permission to drink the milk! And so I did. I drank the milk, washed out the glass, and went back to bed. No big deal.

Next morning we had prayers all together, as we usually did. As we were beginning, I said, "Let's bow our heads and wait before the Lord, to see if there's anything in our hearts that would stand between us and God." The instant I bowed my head I saw, in my mind's eye, a glass of milk. And I heard an inner voice say, "You stole it. Ask for forgiveness."

Then ensued a lengthy but silent discussion between me and God. I had a lot of what seemed to me strong arguments as to why I *should not* confess what I had done. It was such a silly little thing. It would seem so petty. It wouldn't be good for the new Christians to see me make such a big deal of it. It would make them lose respect for me. And so on.

God didn't seem impressed with my reasoning. He just kept saying, "You stole it. Ask for forgiveness. Don't explain it, and don't make excuses, just confess."

After about fifteen minutes of this internal debate—during which everyone else was getting more than a little restless and uncomfortable—I finally gave in. I can't tell you how difficult this was for me to do. Human pride hates to be bashed, or even dinted.

"I have something to say," I said at last. "I have stolen from this community." I didn't offer any complex explanations and I didn't try to justify myself. I just described what had happened, admitted that I had sinned, and asked the group to forgive me.

And did they ever! Everyone just poured on the forgiveness. They were so deeply touched that I, as their leader, would humble myself and admit I had done something wrong. A big deal? On the one hand, no. But on the other hand, my confession made a powerful impression on those young people.

This little incident made a powerful impression on me as well. I came to realize that a thief is a thief—whether he steals five hundred dollars or five cents. It's not the amount, but the act that counts. I also came to realize how important it was to be open to God's voice of correction—and to respond to it quickly when we hear it.

POP QUIZZES BEFORE THE FINAL EXAM

In studying the Scriptures and observing God at work in our lives, I have noticed a number of common tests that the Lord puts people through. God's fundamental agenda for all of us is essentially the same: wanting to bring us to be like Jesus. And while each of us feels utterly unique, all of our human weaknesses are remarkably similar. God wants to establish certain qualities in all of us, and tends to use certain sorts of tests to establish those qualities.

The Test of Rejection. Have you ever noticed how often God's servants are rejected by the very people they came to serve? Joseph was rejected by his brothers. All the prophets were rejected by the people of Israel. Even Jesus "came to his own home, and his own people received him not" (Jn 1:11).

The ability to withstand rejection seems to be an unavoidable prerequisite for serving the Lord. And not just to withstand it, but to persevere through it and choose to love the very ones who are rejecting us. As we pass the test and forgive those who reject us, we grow in our trust of God, and in our determination to persevere to the end. Ninety percent of success is enduring to the end!

The Test of Isolation. Who or what do you need to have in order to get through the day? Familiar surroundings? Friends? Your favorite music? Or is it enough for you to have God, and God alone? I heard of one prominent church official who wouldn't go on weekend retreats or conferences unless he knew for sure he could get his copy of the *New York Times* delivered there!

If we cannot be true to God while trapped in a dungeon—totally isolated from other people, away from our possessions and our familiar surroundings—then our dependence is not really on God but on these other things. So the Lord often creates circumstances of isolation and loneliness to wean us away from our other "support systems."

The Test of Loss of Reputation. The fact is that if our reputation, our "good name," our respectability in the eyes of the world, are too important to us, then God knows he cannot fully trust us. We will also not fully trust him: we will always be inclined to put our own honor ahead of God's. And so he puts us in situations where we are turned into "fools for Christ," until we learn to care more about what God thinks of us than about what other people think.

The Loss of Rights. *This is a test that the Lord seems to apply with special vigor.* Ours is such a rights-oriented society. We define everything in terms of rights. We claim a right to privacy, a right to self-determination, a right to happiness. We don't *ask* for what we feel we need so much as we *demand* it —and God help the person who infringes on our rights.

Often, however, *God* is the person who infringes on our rights! He wants to drive home the fundamental truth that the kingdom of God is not a constitutional democracy, but an absolute monarchy. He is the King! Our time, our money, our privacy—all the things we so defiantly call "ours"—really are not ours at all. They are God's. And he reserves the right to do with them as he sees fit.

It is really very unwise for us to go to God and demand what is rightfully ours. Never demand what you deserve—he might give it to you! The only posture for us to take before God is one of humility: not "standing on our rights" but falling on our faces, gratefully accepting the gift of eternal life and of intimate friendship that God graciously offers us.

Even Jesus "did not count equality with God a thing to be grasped, but emptied himself, taking the form of a servant" (Phil 2:6-7). In the same way, God wants to bring us to a place where we are willing to lay down our "rights" for the sake of his service.

There are many other tests: obedience, humility, hearing and obeying God's voice, preferring one another. But the tests mentioned above are the ones I notice God applying most often and most vigorously!

WHO TURNED OUT THE LIGHTS?

We should consider one other common kind of testing which is certain to come to every Christian sooner or later (and probably both sooner *and* later!). It is the testing we experience when we are walking with God in friendship and suddenly feel as though we're walking alone, as though God had somehow turned away from us.

This sudden feeling of estrangement has been called by different names. Winkey Pratney wrote an excellent article on the subject entitled, "Walking in Darkness: Trusting When You Cannot See."[1] St. John of the Cross wrote an entire book about it, *The Dark Night of the Soul*. A.B. Tozer called it "the ministry of the night." Spurgeon preached about it as "the child of light walking in darkness."

The Scriptures speak of darkness in a number of different senses. There is the black darkness of sin, when men and women choose to hide wicked deeds rather than be exposed by the light of God (see Jn 3:19). There is the darkness of alienation from God, who is the light of the world (see 1 Jn 1:5). Sometimes demons are referred to as "the powers of darkness" (see Lk 22:53; Acts 26:18; Eph 6:12).

Then there is the kind of darkness we are speaking of now: an inexplicable loss of certainty, a withdrawal of the awareness of God's presence—apart from anything we ourselves may have done or failed to do. We suddenly feel as though we have been sucked into some celestial black hole from which no light can escape. From time to time, this darkness seems to fall on every Christian man and woman—regardless of how holy they may be.

Perhaps you have experienced it yourself. You wake up one morning and all your spiritual feelings are gone. You pray, but nothing happens. You rebuke the devil, but it doesn't change anything. You go through all your spiritual exercises and gymnastics. You have your friends pray for you. You confess every sin you can imagine, then go around asking forgiveness of everyone you know. You fast in an effort to make God come back (or, as one person put it, you go on a hunger strike). Still nothing.

You begin to wonder how long this spiritual gloom might last. Days? Weeks? Months? Will it *ever* end? In the meantime, you feel like you're just going through the motions. You go to church and take notes on the sermon. You go to Sunday school and try to participate in the discussions. You listen to tapes. You read books. You think perhaps you can catch God's attention by a demonstration of humility, but when you get on your knees and pray, it feels as if your prayers simply bounce off the ceiling.

In utter desperation, you cry out, "What's the matter with

me?" The answer: *nothing*. What you are experiencing has happened to every man or woman of God at some point. All the heroes of the faith in the Bible went through it. It happened to Abraham while he was waiting for God to accept his sacrifice (Gn 15:12). It happened to Moses on the mountaintop, where he waited to receive the commandments in the "thick darkness" (Dt 5:22). It happened to Job (a spectacularly excruciating case of it, by the way) when he went through his time of testing (Jb 30:26). It happened to David on numerous occasions when it seemed the bottom had dropped out of his world.

What do we do when we find ourselves going through this kind of testing? First, it is important to recognize what we must *not* do. Isaiah paints the picture vividly: "Who among you fears the LORD/ and obeys the voice of his servant,/ who walks in darkness/ and has no light,/ yet trusts in the name of the LORD/ and relies upon his God?/ Behold, all you who kindle a fire,/ who set brands alight!/ Walk by the light of your fire,/ and by the brands you have kindled!/ This shall you have from my hand:/ you shall lie down in torment" (Is 50:10-11).

This passage speaks of people who are walking with God, who fear the Lord and obey, but who are walking in darkness rather than light. What are they tempted to do? To kindle their *own* light! To take matters into their own hands. But what is the fruit of such efforts? Only greater torment. Isaiah is warning us not to kindle our own light, but to simply wait on God until he restores the light.

Many Christians seem to be committed to the Lord largely because of the nice feelings they get. So when a time of darkness comes to them, their immediate reaction is to get busy trying to manufacture more of those fuzzy feelings. Go to a conference! Listen to a tape! Get prayed over. Read more of the Bible.

But it doesn't work. St. John of the Cross offers this instruction:

> The way in which they are to conduct themselves in this night is not to devote themselves to reasoning and meditation, since this is not the time for it; but to allow the soul to remain in peace and quietness, although it may seem clear to them that they are doing nothing and are wasting their time; and, although it may appear to them that it is because of their weakness that they have no desire to think of anything, the truth is that they will be doing quite sufficient if they have patience and persevere in prayer without making any effort.

I have come across believers who were in the midst of a "dark night of the soul." Some of them said, "Well, if God isn't going to speak to me, then I'll just have to go ahead and make a decision. I'll just have to step out and do my best and let him stop me if I'm making a mistake."

What are they really saying? "Okay, God, if you're not going to guide me, I'll just guide myself. If you won't speak, I'll speak myself. If you won't build a fire, I'll build my own fire."

Such wasted efforts only serve to intensify the blackness. As Pratney says, "Don't make the foolish and futile mistake of lighting your own fire. If God has put you in the darkness, let it do its work in your soul. He got you in; you can trust him to take you out."[2]

What is the purpose of this kind of darkness? To build us into men and women of God, disciples who are not dependent on circumstances, or feelings, or spiritual formulas, or anything else... *but who will wait for God no matter what the cost.*

Unfortunately, most of us don't appreciate the light we have when God *is* guiding us and speaking to us and feeding us by his Word and revealing his presence to us. Each of us desperately needs to go through these periods of darkness in order to cultivate both a sensitivity to what is and is not God's light, and to deepen our appreciation for the bright light from heaven bestowed on the friends of God.

NOT A TIME TO TWIDDLE OUR THUMBS

Here are some things we *should* do in the darkness. First, we should carry on with the last thing God showed us to do. Old orders remain God's orders. Second, we should remember that other men and women of God have been through the same experience—and have not only survived it but grown stronger through it. Finally, we should remember that "God is the one who dwells in thick darkness" (Dt 5:22). He is there with us, in the midst of the testing.

Remember: like all God's discipline and testing, this darkness is meant for our good. And this black canopy will not be withdrawn until it has accomplished the purpose for which it was intended. The Bible tells us of Jacob, who "was left alone; and a man wrestled with [him] until the breaking of the day" (Gn 32:24). That is what we, too, must do: *cling to God until he leads us through the darkness, even when we seem to be holding on for dear life.*

I remember one young man who became a Christian through our ministry in Afghanistan many years ago. When he came to us, he told us he was committed to seeking the truth no matter where the search led him. He eventually came to a point where he was convinced that Christianity was the truth. But when he looked inside himself, he realized that he in fact did not really want to surrender his life to God. He was so disappointed in himself that he contemplated suicide.

Then this man decided to simply trust God in spite of his

feelings. He said, "It's the truth, and I will choose to believe it whether I feel like it or not; I will follow God whether I *ever* feel his presence or not." He went for several months devoid of any inner sense of the presence of God.

His was an extraordinary case: a new Christian actually *born* into a time of testing and darkness. I don't think I've ever seen it happen since. But God was faithful. In due course, God *did* make himself known. That young man's decision to "hang in there" was a remarkable act of integrity and was the foundation on which he was able to build his Christian life.

I believe God has five main objectives when he tests us:

1. To strengthen our character.
2. To spur our growth as his friend.
3. To reconcile us with others from whom we are estranged.
4. To set us free from any sin that holds us in bondage.
5. To teach us his ways.

We need to relinquish the idea that God's testing is punishment. It isn't. When God disciplines us and tests us, it is not because he is *against* us, but precisely because he is *for* us. God never tests us in order to hurt us, but in order to help us. He never tests us in order to destroy us, but in order to build us up. He never tests us in order to wound us, but in order to heal us. With God, the "friendly fire" is always the fire of love—one more opportunity to find more intimate friendship with God.

11

The Friend Who Listens

WHEN SALLY WAS BORN, her mother was forty-seven years old. She already had four children from her first marriage, and when her first husband died she married a man with four of his own. Most people would have assumed she was done raising her family. But she had always wanted one of her children to be a missionary, and none of her eight kids seemed inclined in that direction. So she prayed that the Lord would send her one more.

Two days after this last little baby was born, her mother took Sally into the tiny church she attended in Galveston, Texas, laid her on the altar, and dedicated her to God. She made a vow to pray every day for her little girl, that she would hear God's call to the mission field. That's how certain she was that God had given Sally to her for that purpose.

One night when Sally was five years old, she awoke in the middle of the night, crying. All she could think about was a family from their church who were missionaries to Africa. The more she thought about them, she more she cried. She woke her mother and told her what was happening. Her mother—immediately perceiving that it was the Holy Spirit at work in her little girl—told her to go back to bed and pray for the missionary family. Sally later remembered that she finally drifted off to sleep thinking, "Some day I'm going to be just like them."

When Sally was sixteen, the opportunity arose for her to go on a summer outreach to the island of Samoa. However, several barriers barred the way. For one thing, the sponsors of the trip didn't want to take anyone who wasn't at least eighteen years old. For another, her stepfather—who was not a Christian—didn't want her to go. And last but not least, it cost a lot of money to go on the outreach, a tidy sum totally out of the teenager's reach.

Two weeks before the trip was to begin, Sally's stepfather told her he had changed his mind. She was flabbergasted: she had been pleading with him every week for months to give her permission to go, and he had been adamant in his refusal. Now, suddenly, he said she could go.

Why the about-face? Apparently, he assumed that since Sally didn't have enough money, she wouldn't be able to go even if she did have his permission; by saying yes he could avoid looking like the bad guy. Little did he know that while Sally didn't have the full amount she needed, she had managed to scrape together enough to get to Los Angeles, where the week-long training session for the outreach trip was to be held. Much to her stepfather's chagrin (and to her mother's delight), off she went.

In Los Angeles, Sally ran head-on into the sponsors of the trip, who told her she couldn't go. They pointed out that she was below the minimum age they had established. They also pointed out that she didn't have any money to pay for her food, lodging, and transportation.

There was a young man in Sally's training course who had also grown up wanting to be a missionary, and who had been working and saving for months so he could go on this outreach to Samoa. During the course of the week he and Sally got to know each other. She told him of her conviction that the Lord wanted her to go on the trip, and of her confidence that the Lord would somehow make it possible.

One night as he was praying, the young man sensed the Lord speaking to him. The Lord seemed to be saying, "Give her your money. You are to stay home so that she can go." Since that definitely wasn't what he wanted to hear, he argued the point at some length.

His arguments seemed sound. He was between his second and third year of university and might never have the freedom to make such a trip again. He had worked hard to save up the money. He believed God had called him years before to be a missionary, and this was going to be his first overseas adventure.

But God was not to be dissuaded. Finally, the night before the group was to leave, the young man went to the sponsors and told them what he had decided.

Now the sponsors found themselves in a predicament. It had been easy for them to stick to their guns regarding Sally's age so long as they knew she didn't have the money for the trip anyway. But now that obstacle had been overcome. And Sally—who still knew nothing of the young man's decision— was as determined as ever.

The morning the group was to leave, the sponsors called the teenager on the telephone. "What are you doing right now, Sally?" they asked.

"Packing to go to Samoa," she exclaimed.

"But we told you you can't go," they said.

"I know what you told me," Sally said. "But the Lord has given me faith to trust him. I believe I'm supposed to go to the airport—right up to the door of the plane, if necessary—and that if I do, he'll make a way for me. Somehow I believe he'll change your minds, as well as take care of my finances."

The sponsors were amazed and encouraged by Sally's response. What could anyone say to faith like that? "Look, Sally," they said. "Last night someone came forward and provided the money for you to go. And we've prayed about it, and... well, we feel this is a sign that we should make an exception and let you go."

And go she did. Sally's group spent most of the summer in a small village where no missionaries had ever been able to visit before. In fact, when they first arrived, a local leader told them they could go to any other village on the island but that one. He encouraged them to pray and ask the Lord where else they should go. Naturally, the Lord said, "Go to the village he told you that you couldn't get into. I'll get you in."

They did, and God did, and by the end of the summer one hundred fifty of that village's three hundred inhabitants—including the chief—had become Christians. Today, the church those young people started is the largest one of its denomination on the whole island.

Needless to say, the whole incident made a profound impact on Sally. It made a profound impact on the young man as well. Seeing the amazing circumstances—the way his decision about giving away his money changed the sponsors' minds about letting Sally go—convinced him that he really had heard the Lord. God rewarded Sally's obedience, and he rewarded the young man as well. The experience persuaded him, once and for all, that the Lord really does speak today, and that he wants his people to listen. It opened up a whole new area of the spiritual realm to him.

The reason I know so much about this story is that the young man was *me*. And Sally is now my wife.

MONOLOGUE OR DIALOGUE

I think one of the things I appreciate most in a friend is his or her ability to listen. Sally is a good listener. She's also my best friend. I love sharing my dreams and ideas with her. I've been in working relationships with some people who dominated the conversation every time we were together. After an hour or more of nonstop monologue on their part, my patience with them begins to run thin! But Sally has really been an example to me of a person who listens to God—and to people.

Have you ever seen folks who *act* like they are listening when they really aren't? They're just going through the motions, waiting until you finish speaking so they can say what they were going to say anyway. They're not really making an effort to connect with you, to understand what is really on your mind and in your heart.

I myself have not, historically, been a very good listener. In fact, it is just in the last few years that the Lord has really impressed on me the importance of taking time to hear people out and make sure I understand their point of view. I tend to be one of those folks who knows what he wants to say before the other person has had a chance to finish. To some degree, I think this comes from serving for so many years in a leadership/management role, relating to people primarily as a problem-solver. *Let's get on with things. We've got a lot to do. Don't waste my time with a lot of blather.*

One of my main lessons in the school of listening came through an encounter with my wife. Sally had been sharing with me some struggles she was going through. After she finished, I ticked off three things I thought she ought to do to straighten things out. Sally looked up at me and said, "I already *know* what I need to do. I wasn't coming to you for a three-step answer. I was coming to you for some understanding, some comfort. If I can't talk to *you*, who *can* I talk to?"

Those words resounded in my head for days afterwards. *If I can't talk to you, who can I talk to?* I made up my mind then and there to be the kind of husband Sally *could* talk to—and to be the kind of friend that other people could talk to, as well.

Somewhere in the midst of this particular lesson, it suddenly occurred to me: if we human beings have such a strong need to be listened to, to be understood, in our relationships with one another, how much *more* true must this be in our relationship with God?

If we are going to be friends with God, surely listening is going to be an important part of the picture. God is the kind of friend who listens—to each one of us individually. He wants us, in turn, to be the kind of friends who listen, too—to our heavenly Father as well as to one another.

I grew up in a home where listening to God was constantly modeled for me. As a pioneer church planter, my dad was a strong believer in the importance of spending time talking and listening to God. Many were the times I would walk down the hallway in our house and hear his voice filtering through the bedroom door, calling out the names of men and women in the church, asking the Lord to show him what he, as their pastor, should be doing for them.

At other times, Dad would go to church on a Friday afternoon and spend the whole weekend there in prayer. His Sunday morning preaching would be borne out of that time spent before the Lord. I remember going for many a family drive and, when things got quiet, hearing my father quietly talking—to God.

For my dad, prayer wasn't just a matter of spending a predetermined amount of time rattling off a series of rote words. It was a dynamic, living thing. You could do it anywhere, anytime, in any position. You didn't have to be kneeling. And you didn't just talk, you also listened. You assumed that God would want to speak to you, so you made a point of listening for his voice.

I can't remember a time when conversing with God was not an important part of my life. Because of my parents' example, I knew that I could talk to God about any problem or need that I faced.

When I was in high school, I wasn't allowed to participate in a lot of the clubs and social activities (our church was very conservative and such things were forbidden). As a result, I often felt as though I were "on the outside looking in." I can still remember the many walks home from school when I would pour out my feelings of insecurity and frustration to the Lord. I look back with deep thankfulness to God that I could talk to him about my hurts and disappointments; that is the kind of God he is: the kind who would want to hear about my troubles, who would want to talk to me about them.

A GOD WHO SPEAKS

But does God *really* speak to us? Or does he just listen? And *how* does he do it? Do we have to wait hours, days, weeks, or years to hear God speak to us? Or is there the possibility of a more immediate response?

Can God put a new idea directly into our minds? Can he give us a new perspective as an answer to our prayers? Can he change our old, faulty desires into new, godly ones? Can he calm turbulent emotions? Can he stimulate certain memories in our minds when those recollections are needed? Can he speak into our imaginations and dreams? Can God actually whisper into listening ears?

I believe the answer to all these questions is an emphatic *yes.* My conviction—based on years of experience on top of what the Bible teaches—is that God himself actually puts his own ideas into our minds, when we listen carefully to his voice. I believe he shares his perspectives with us, widens our vision, helps us see what is really important to him, helps us separate the truly important from the merely urgent. I believe God comes to us in our listening moments and speaks to us.

There are some Christians—you may well have run into them—who do not believe that God speaks to us in this way. They would say that he has spoken to us through his Son, Jesus, and through his revealed Word, the Bible—that these sources give us everything we need for "teaching, for reproof, for correction, and for training in righteousness" (2 Tm 3:16). These Christians would say that God speaks to us today solely through the Scriptures.

I respect such people, but I disagree with them. Or rather, I believe that while what they say is true, it is not *all* of the truth.

I would estimate that 80 to 90 percent of the decisions I make are guided purely by scriptural principles. For example, if I'm praying about two jobs, and one of them involves dishonesty, I immediately know to reject it. I don't need a special word from the Lord to tell me not to be dishonest; it is a basic biblical principle. But while the Bible may tell me to reject the second job, it doesn't necessarily tell me that I *should* take the first one. Maybe the Lord has another job in mind for me, one that I'm not yet aware of.

But a great many of the choices and decisions we face involve two or three or more options—all of which seem perfectly fine and none of which is clearly ruled out by scriptural principles. What do we do in such instances? Do we assume that God simply has no opinion on the matter? Or is it rather the case that he does have wisdom for us? If so, how might he communicate this advice to us?

I believe that the Bible itself tells us that God *does* want to speak to us directly, and that it gives us many examples of how he goes about doing so. He is our friend and he wants to commune with us. Jesus said, "I am the good shepherd; I know my own and my own know me.... And I have other sheep, that are not of this fold; I must bring them also, and they will heed my voice" (Jn 10:14-16).

Peter quotes the promise God gave through the prophet Joel, that in times to come "... I will pour out my Spirit upon all flesh,/ and your sons and your daughters shall prophesy,/ and your young men shall see visions,/ and your old men shall dream dreams" (Acts 2:17). Paul repeats the same concept when he enumerates the gifts of the Spirit, some of which are essentially gifts of communication: prophecy, tongues, discernment, wisdom, and knowledge (see 1 Cor 12).

All through the Scriptures, we see God speaking with human beings in very personal ways. Adam and Eve walked and talked with God in the cool of the day (see Gn 3:8). Abraham heard the Lord speak to him on many occasions (for example, see Gn 17:1). We read that "the LORD used to speak to Moses face to face, as a man speaks to his friend" (Ex 33:11). God spoke to Samuel (see 1 Sm 3:8-10), to the prophets (see Is 44:1 and Is 55:2), and to many, many other biblical figures.

God is described as speaking in a variety of ways. He speaks through dreams, visions, and angels. He speaks through nature, through the counsel of godly friends, even through the taunts of our enemies. One time he even spoke through a donkey! (See Numbers 22:21-41.)

Clearly, God wants to speak to us; God is *able* to speak to us; and he wants us to be alert to his voice. The command God gave to Peter, James, and John on the Mount of Transfiguration, he also gives to us: "This is my beloved Son, with whom I am well pleased; *listen to him*" (Mt 17:5; italics mine).

Our friendship with God—just like our friendship with anyone else—grows through communication. Our relationship will stagnate if we do not remember that God is a friend who listens, and if we do not ourselves become friends who listen to him as well.

Someone once made the observation that an experienced surgeon will operate on a patient more swiftly and surely than will a medical student who has to keep referring to a textbook. And that in just the same way, an habitually prayerful person will hear and discern God's voice more quickly and accurately than one who spends time listening to God only sporadically.

How tragic that many Christians miss out on this tremendous aspect of relationship with God—the comfort of being able to speak with him, and the excitement of hearing their heavenly Father speak in return. Perhaps they have never even known it was possible. Perhaps they have tried it, fleetingly and feebly, and simply given up when their efforts didn't seem to pay off.

In my own case, I have concluded that when I am *not* hearing God's voice, it is usually a sign that there is something wrong, some blockage in me that the Lord wants to remove... unless I happen to be passing through one of those dark nights of the soul. Listening to the Lord has been one of the greatest adventures of my life.

A RISKY RIDE THROUGH THE RAPIDS

But how do I know—how can *you* know—that it is really *God* who is speaking? This, of course, is the big question. If we are wrong on this point—if we are going around listening to voices that aren't his—we could be in real trouble.

There are, in essence, three voices that we might hear

speaking to us when we pray. The first, of course, is the voice of the Lord. The second is our own "voice," the thoughts and imaginations of our own mind and heart. The third is the voice of the evil one, who would like nothing better than to steer us astray.

Let's consider these three possibilities in reverse order. In seeking the voice of the Lord, the worst-case scenario is that we instead hear the voice of the devil. Let me say immediately that this is not something we need to worry about as much as our fears might suggest—if we remain open to correction and have a humble heart and if we are committed to testing any guidance we receive by God's written Word. There are several reasons why I say this. The first is the promise of Jesus:

> "Ask, and it will be given you; seek, and you will find; knock, and it will be opened to you. For every one who asks receives, and he who seeks finds, and to him who knocks it will be opened. What father among you, if his son asks for a fish, will instead of a fish give him a serpent...? If you then, who are evil, know how to give good gifts to your children, how much more will the heavenly Father give the Holy Spirit to those who ask him?" **Lk 11:9-13**

Jesus speaks these words while teaching his disciples about prayer. They assure us that if we go to the Lord and ask him to speak to us, he will not let the evil one lead us astray.

Moreover, Scripture tells us that we have authority over the work of the devil, that if we resist him and submit to God, he will flee from us (see Jas 4:7). Thus we can say, "I resist you, Satan in Jesus' name," and be confident that he will not interfere with our ability to hear the Lord's voice clearly.

What about the possibility that our own thoughts and desires will get in the way? Our protection here is to make a conscious, deliberate choice to die to our own hopes and dreams and desires, and to tell the Lord we desire that only *his* will, not ours, be done.

We can simply say, "Lord, I don't want my imagination or my emotions to get in the way of hearing your voice," and trust him to honor that prayer. We can pray with confidence, "Lord Jesus, I believe that you want to speak to me, that your thoughts are higher than my thoughts and your ways higher than my ways, and that you want to instruct me. So I come before you in child-like faith, trusting that the thoughts and perspectives that form in my mind are from you."

Sound risky? It is. But living by faith is always risky, by definition. I myself have practiced this simple approach for more than twenty-five years. Talking to the Lord and expecting him to speak to me in return has become a way of life for me. I have made mistakes, of course. But over the years I have learned to listen to the Lord—and, as with anything else, the more you practice something, the better you're able to do it. *Our protection lies in being obedient to God's revealed Word, the Bible, and in being accountable in all our decisions to other believers.*

There are some concrete steps we can take to make this risky process more reliable. One is to have several friends who can act as counselors or mentors—close friends with whom you can share what you believe the Lord is saying to you, who can help confirm if God is speaking to you. It will be well worth your time and effort to seek out such persons and establish a trusting relationship with them.

Second, it is important to set aside uncluttered, unencumbered time to be alone with God. Try this: schedule a day or two to go to a retreat center (or even to a nearby hotel or motel) all by yourself. Take along some spiritual books to read or some tapes to listen to, if that will help; but make it a goal to spend a majority of your time simply listening to the Lord in the manner described earlier. You may find it helpful to read the Scriptures and pray out loud what you are reading. Expect God to quicken his Word to your heart and apply it personally to your situation.

Third, study the Scriptures, especially those that concern the ways God wants to speak to us. The passages I have cited in this chapter will give you a place to start. You can also find many books and tapes on the subject. My own book, *Basic Discipleship*,[1] offers a more detailed treatment of this whole topic. Even a concordance can help you look up references to God speaking, to God's voice, to prophecy, angels, visions, dreams, and so on.

Finally, remember what I said about the importance of practice. Let me suggest that each time you face a decision of any significance in the days and weeks ahead, you pause and take the following steps.

- Tell the Lord that you die to your own thoughts and desires, and be totally surrendered to his will for your life.
- Resist the devil; command him to flee from you.
- Tell the Lord in faith that you believe he wants to speak to you, and that he *will* speak to you.
- Ask your question of God and wait quietly. Trust that he will give you a thought or impression, either right then, or in the days or weeks to come.
- Ask him to confirm what he has said to you through Scripture and through the counsel of godly people in the days and weeks ahead.

I believe that the more you practice listening to the Lord, the more you will hear him speak to you. You will receive help with the choices and decisions that face you. And you will experience greater confidence in your daily life.

Most of all, you will grow in intimacy with God. He will

comfort you in times of trouble, guide you in important decisions, and impart wisdom for difficult situations. You will grow closer to your heavenly Father as you open your heart to him, asking his counsel for the difficulties you face. You will experience his intimate concern for you as you share your deepest secrets and greatest longings.

God is a friend who listens. He invites you to draw closer to him as he shares with you the desires of *his* heart.

In one sense, this entire book is about hearing from God. The one message he wants to get through to every person on this planet is his immense and unending commitment to love us and be our friend.

But God needs to hear from each one of us. He reaches out to us, but we must respond.

God is waiting to hear from you right now. Has this book stirred your heart to be a friend of God? Have you found pathways through the pages of this book that lead you to deeper friendship with God?

Won't you take time, right now, to tell God how much you want to be his friend, that you respond to his love and accept his gift of friendship?

Notes

ONE
Knowing God

1. Thomas F. Torrance, *Theological Science* (London: Oxford University Press, 1969), 73-74.
2. C.S. Lewis, *The Problem of Pain* (New York, New York: Macmillan, 1978), 16.

TWO
What a Friend We Have in Jesus

1. From *Inspiring Hymns* (Grand Rapids, Michigan: Singspiration Music, Zondervan Corporation, 1982).

FOUR
God's Plan for the Ages

1. Jerry Bridges, *Transforming Grace* (Colorado Springs, Colorado: NavPress, 1991), 61.

FIVE
Religion: A Case of Mistaken Identity

1. David Needham, *Birthright* (Portland, Oregon: Multnomah, 1979), 47.

SIX
True Identity: Who Are We, Really?

1. Needham, *Birthright*, 48.
2. Bob George, *Growing in Grace*.

SEVEN
Nine Barriers to Friendship with God

1. Floyd McClung, *Holiness and the Spirit of the Age* (Eugene, Oregon: Harvest House Publishers, 1990), 77.
2. Alice Poynor, "A Simple Holiness: The Life of Hudson Taylor," *Discipleship Journal*, Issue 49, 1989, 31.
3. Poynor, 32.

TEN
Friendly Fire

1. I highly recommend this article by Winkey Pratney, which can be found in *Last Days* magazine, Vol. 14, No. 3, 19.
2. Pratney, 19.

ELEVEN
The Friend Who Listens

1. Floyd McClung, *Basic Discipleship* (Downers Grove, Illinois: InterVarsity Press, 1992). Available in UK as *Wholehearted* (London: Marshall Pickering, 1992).

For further information concerning
Youth With a Mission
write to the following address:

Youth With A Mission
13 Highfield Oval
Ambrose Lane
Harpenden
Herts AL5 4BX
Tel: 0582 765481
Fax: 0582 768048